William Francis Hutchinson

Under the Southern Cross

A guide to the sanitariums and other charming places in the West Indies and

Spanish Main

William Francis Hutchinson

Under the Southern Cross
A guide to the sanitariums and other charming places in the West Indies and Spanish Main

ISBN/EAN: 9783337254117

Printed in Europe, USA, Canada, Australia, Japan

Cover: Foto ©Andreas Hilbeck / pixelio.de

More available books at **www.hansebooks.com**

UNDER THE SOUTHERN CROSS.

A GUIDE TO THE SANITARIUMS AND OTHER CHARMING
PLACES IN THE WEST INDIES AND SPANISH MAIN.

BY

WILLIAM F. HUTCHINSON, A. M., M. D.,

FELLOW AMERICAN CLIMATOLOGICAL SOCIETY, MEMBER
AMERICAN MEDICAL ASSOCIATION, MEMBER
AMERICAN PUBLIC HEALTH AS-
SOCIATION, ETC., ETC.

ILLUSTRATIONS FROM

AUTHOR'S SKETCHES AND PHOTOGRAPHS

PROVIDENCE:
THE RYDER & DEARTH CO.
1891.

Entered according to Act of Congress in the year 1891, by W. F. HUTCHINSON, in the office of the Librarian of Congress, Washington, D. C.

"Land ho, in the sunset! All hail, Happy Islands!
　We sail through their shadows: we scent their perfume.
　O beaches of silver! O emerald highlands!
　　O valleys immortal of fruitage and bloom!"

CONTENTS.

Chapter I.

THE DIFFICULTY OF SELECTING A CLIMATE — SAD EXPERIENCES AT ST. EUSTATIUS — WHAT IS NEEDED IN NEW PLACES — GENERAL METEOROLOGICAL HINTS — NOTES OF FOOD AND WATER — REMEDIES FOR SEA SICKNESS — RATES OF FARE. . . . . Page 7.

Chapter II.

WHY WARM CLIMATES ARE BEST — SOME FORMS OF DISEASE CURED BY THE TROPICS — MEANS OF AMUSEMENT — EFFECTS OF STEADY HEAT — INCREASE AND LOSS OF WEIGHT, ... Page 17.

Chapter III.

WHAT CLASSES OF INVALIDS SHOULD AVOID TROPICAL COUNTRIES — THE ISLANDS BAD FOR RHEUMATISM — HINTS ABOUT CLOTHING NEEDED THERE — CAUTION IN EATING DEMANDED — SUGGESTIONS FOR DIET — CHOICE OF PHYSICIAN WHEN NECESSARY, Page 28.

CONTENTS.

Chapter IV.

TAKE PLENTY OF LUGGAGE — THE WAY THAT LAUNDRY WORK IS DONE — CHEAP GOWNS AND HEAD WEAR FOR LADIES — LITTLE SABA, "NAPOLEON'S COCKED HAT" — FIRST IMPRESSIONS OF ST. KITTS — DRIVES AND HOTELS THERE — WHERE LORD NELSON WAS MARRIED — NEVIS AND THE BATH, . Page 36.

Chapter V.

ANTIGUA — DOMINICA.

GREEN TURTLE DINNERS AT ANTIGUA — THE VALLEY OF PETRIFACTIONS — THE PUBLIC LIBRARY — A VISIT TO ENGLISH HARBOR — SOME NOTES ON THE GEOLOGY AND CLIMATE OF ANTIGUA — ABOUT THE STREETS OF ST. JOHN'S — ACCOMMODATIONS IN HOTELS AND BOARDING HOUSES — WHAT THERE IS TO EAT — AMUSEMENTS — CLUBS AND HOSPITALITY — NO YELLOW FEVER — HOW DOMINICA GOT ITS NAME — THE MOST BEAUTIFUL SCENERY IN THE ISLANDS — TO THE BOILING SPRINGS — WHAT THE CURIOS ARE — STORY OF THE BOILING LAKE — WHERE TO CATCH GREY MULLET — DR. NICHOL'S ACCOUNT OF CARIBS. . . . . . . Page 44.

Chapter VI.

THE FRENCH ISLANDS.

CHARM IN CHANGING NATIONS — CURIOUS DEVELOPMENT OF SPECIAL CHARACTERISTICS — A MARTINIQUIEN FOUR TIMES A FRENCHMAN — AN EPITOME OF EUROPE — ADVENTURES OF FOUR TOURISTS — NO CHARGE FOR WINE — MASONIC TEMPLE AT GUA-

CONTENTS.

DELOUPE — HEALTH OF THAT ISLAND — NO MODERN CONVENIENCES — CHARMING BITS FOR ARTISTS — BOATS IN THE BAY OF ST. PIERRE — HOTEL CHARGES — CENTIPEDES AND OTHER VERMIN — THE FONTAINES CHAUDES — A FAIR MARTINIQUIENNE — STATUE AND HOME OF JOSEPHINE — THE IRON LANCE — TROIS ISLETS POTTERY. . . Page 58.

CHAPTER VII.
BARBADOS.

CHARACTER OF THE LAND — CROWDED POPULATION — EXCELLENT HOTELS, THEIR LOCATION AND RATES — DRAINAGE OF THE ISLAND — ITS UNVARYING TEMPERATURE — BEAUTY OF APPROACH TO LAND — ENTRANCE TO CARLISLE BAY — CHARACTER OF NEGROES — VARIETY OF FOOD SUPPLIES — HOW STRANGERS MAY LIVE BEST — CHARMING DRIVES AND LUXURIOUS SEA BATHS — HOW SUGAR CANE GROWS — A CHARMING HOUR OF EARLY MORNING — ALONG THE NORTH COAST BY RAIL — NO REPTILES NOR INSECTS — THE ANIMAL FLOWER CAVE — CHEAP CLOTHING FOR BOTH SEXES — BRILLIANT SUNSETS — SKILFUL MEDICAL MEN. . . Page 72.

CHAPTER VIII.
TRINIDAD.

"QUE ISLA GLORIOSA!" — GREAT VARIETY OF SURFACE AND LARGE AREA — WONDERFUL TREE FERNS AND ORCHIDS — SOME OF THE HOTELS — 'WARE BOAT AND CABMEN! — HOW HOT IT IS — PECULIARITIES OF SOCIETY — DRAMATIC HARBOR APPROACH — NEED OF

CONTENTS.

GOOD LETTERS OF INTRODUCTION — THE HINDU TOWN AND BLUE BASIN — SHOPS OF PORT OF SPAIN AND WHAT THEY CONTAIN — COURTESIES OF THE UNION CLUB — A TRIP TO ST. JOSEPH — HOW TO GET TO MARACCAS VALE — THE GREAT PITCH LAKE OF LA BREA — APROPOS OF LEPERS — CAPT. MALING'S STORY OF THE CARIBS — THEIR HABITS AND RELIGIOUS BELIEFS — THE YELLOW AND BLACK CARIBS — PHOTOGRAPHS AND CURIOS — WHERE TO BUY THEM — ANGOSTURA BITTERS, . Page 91.

Chapter IX.

THE SPANISH MAIN.

HOW TO REACH IT — NOTES OF THE ROYAL MAIL BOATS — PUERTO CABELLO AND HER LOVELY SUBURBS — FEATHER FLOWERS AT SANT ESTEBAN — TO LA GUAIRA AND MACUTO — THE WONDERFUL RAILWAY TO CARACAS — THE CAPITAL CITY OF THE INCAS — COOL NIGHTS AND PLEASANT DAYS — COOKS IN CABS — MARDI GRAS AND LA CARNIVAL — COFFEE AND ITS CULTURE — BEWARE OF MILDEW — LARGE AND IMPORTANT FLORA — HOME LIFE IN VENEZUELA — INLAND VALENCIA AND THE LAKE OF TARA YACA — THE NEED OF SOME KNOWLEDGE OF SPANISH — THE RED "D" FLEET — CURAÇAO AND ITS DUTCH PECULIARITIES — SUPERB GROUND FOR ARTISTS — MARACAIBO AND ITS EMPTY STREETS — THE LAKE VILLAGE AT SANTA ROSAS — YOUNG WOMEN FOR SALE — A WONDERFUL INLAND SEA, ... Page 111.

CONTENTS.

CHAPTER X.
COSTA RICA.

ITS UNKNOWN INTERIOR AND HEALTH RESORTS — A CLIMATE OF PERPETUAL SPRING — HOW TO GET THERE — NO HOTELS AT THE SEA PORTS — THE CHARMING VALLEY OF CARTAGO — THE ATLANTIC AND PACIFIC IN ONE VIEW — TEMPERATURE AND ANALYSIS OF MEDICINAL SPRINGS — SAN JOSÉ AND ITS BUILDINGS — AN EVENING WITH THE PEOPLE — EXPENSES HIGHER THAN IN THE ISLANDS — WHAT IT COSTS TO LIVE THERE — NEED FOR GUIDES IN THE FORESTS — CASCADES AND MOUNTAIN CLIMBING — THE VOLCANO OF IRAZU, . . . Page 131.

CHAPTER XI.
JAMAICA.

SCARCITY OF INFORMATION RELATIVE TO THE ISLAND — AMERICAN HOTELS TO BE FOUND — GENEROUS HOSPITALITY OF RESIDENTS — ADVANTAGES TO HEALTH SEEKERS — WHAT AN INVALID NEEDS TO KNOW — CLIMATE RANGES AND TABLES — FIRST IMPRESSIONS OF KINGSTON — BEAUTIFUL VIEWS OF THE BLUE MOUNTAINS — CAPT. WALKER AND THE COASTING STEAMER — A FAMOUS RACONTEUR — THE STORY OF JESS AND SOLOMON'S MINES — DR. PHILLIPPO'S ESTIMATE OF THE CLIMATE — THE MANCHESTER HEIGHTS AND MANDEVILLE — AMERICAN MONEY GOOD IN JAMAICA — WONDERFUL BATHS — SURE CURE FOR RHEUMATISM — LUCEA AND THE PARSON — ANECDOTES OF THE BROWN PEOPLE — MONTEGO BAY AND ITS HOTEL — JAMAICAN LOVE FOR AMERICA — FOOT

CONTENTS.

PRINTS OF COLUMBUS — BÊTE ROUGE — KEEP OFF THE GRASS — ST. ANN'S BAY — THE END OF SPANISH RULE — OBI-ISM IN A POLICE COURT — PORT ANTONIO AND THE MAROONS — TOM CRINGLE'S LOG A GOOD GUIDE — THE RETURN TO KINGSTON, . Page 142.

Chapter XII.
CUBA.

SPANISH OPPRESSION AND CRUELTY — UNSAFE STREETS BY NIGHT IN HAVANA — GENERAL SKETCH OF THE ISLAND — WHY THERE ARE NO LARGE RIVERS — WHERE COFFEE ONCE GREW — THE VUELTA ABAJO — ARRIVAL AT THE CUSTOM DOCK — HOTELS OF HAVANA — TEMPERATURE AND CLOTHING NEEDED — BE CAREFUL WHAT YOU EAT — ALSO WHAT YOU DRINK — REMARKS UPON CUBAN DRINKS IN GENERAL — NOT MUCH ABOUT BULL FIGHTS — A VISIT TO THE FOUNDLING ASYLUM — AND ANOTHER TO THE LEPER HOSPITAL — HOW SUGAR IS MADE AT LA TOLEDO — A RUN DOWN TO MATANZAS — WHO FOUND THE CAVES OF BELLAMAR — A PICTURE OF YUMURRI — ALONG THE SOUTH COAST — CIENFUEGOS AND SANTIAGO — THE ISLE OF PINES, Page 169.

Chapter XIII.
BERMUDA.

BY THE QUEBEC LINE DOWN — FINE SHIPS AND GOOD OFFICERS — SOCIETY AND SPORTS — THE ARRIVAL AT HAMILTON — COMFORTABLE TEMPERATURE — THE ISLAND HOTELS — EXCURSIONS TO BE TAKEN — A MILITARY STATION AND A FASHIONABLE WINTER RESORT.
Page 185.

CONTENTS.

Chapter XIV.
NASSAU.

THE FAMILIAR BAHAMAS — HOW TO REACH THEM — FIRST VIEW OF THE SOUTHERN CROSS — BEAUTIES OF CUBAN SOUTHCOAST SCENERY — FIRST IMPRESSIONS OF NASSAU — EASY CUSTOMS OFFICERS — TO THE SEA GARDENS — LIVERY HIRE AND BOATS — A FIRST TASTE OF TROPICAL FRUIT — WONDERFUL FISHING IN NASSUA HARBOR — NO SUCH SEA BATHING ANYWHERE — THE QUEEN'S STAIRCASE — THE "PREPOSTEROUS" LAKE — A RUSH AT THE SHOUTING CHURCH — INCREASING VALUE OF LAND — ITS GREAT VALUE AS A HEALTH RESORT — A WONDERFUL SANITARIUM FOR NERVES — NOT AN EXPENSIVE PLACE TO LIVE — A FAMOUS NEGRO HYMN — "THE GENERAL ROLL CALL." . . Page 192.

Chapter XV.
THE ORINOCO RIVER.

ITS CACIQUES AND BEAUTIFUL WOMEN OF OLDEN TIME — RALEIGH'S ACCOUNT OF IT — HOW AN AMERICAN GOT THE TRADE — THE "BOLIVAR" AND CAPT. MATHISON — FIRST IMPRESSIONS OF THE RIVER BY NIGHT — BANDS OF GUARAUNO INDIANS — IMMENSE AND SUDDEN RISES OF THE RIVER — AN INDIAN VILLAGE — A FORTY FOOT CAYMAN — AND AN IGUANA — THE FAMOUS GOLD MINES — ARRIVAL AT BOLIVAR — THE "PRISON EDITOR" — GRASS GROWS IN THE STREETS — A SEARCH FOR FEATHER WORK — HEAVY FREIGHTS — BACK OF THE TOWN — THE TRAINED BULL — LOADING CATTLE — PAN! PAN! — END OF THE JOURNEY. Page 207.

PREFACE.

In my many visits to the West Indies and South America, chiefly for health purposes, I have found among fellow-passengers an earnest inquiry for some reliable book of reference — something that would tell them where to go and what to see when arrived.

They have been unable to find anything that does this, except folders and guides of steamship lines, and could learn but little from them.

There is also a large demand in the medical profession for a reliable description of these countries which shall provide information of their respective values as health resorts, and there is no such book.

So I present this volume, hoping that it may, to some extent, fill an empty niche, and do good by attracting intelligent attention to the sanitary value and scenic beauty of the islands of the sun.

It has been prepared with care. Each chapter has been printed in a leading medical journal, submitted to governmental or other official criticism in country or island described, and all corrections from such sources have been made before assembling the book.

If each of the rapidly increasing number of travelers in Southern Seas proves as fortunate as I have been in regaining health and prolonging life in their beneficent atmosphere, he may chance to feel, as I do, a sense of gratitude for the advice that sent him there and of duty to tell to others how much of life and pleasure those countries may have in store for them.

PROVIDENCE, RHODE ISLAND, 1891.

GRAND CASCADE, BOTANICAL GARDENS, MARTINIQUE.

UNDER THE SOUTHERN CROSS.

Chapter I.

THERE is, each year, as often as winter comes around, a steadily increasing number of Americans traveling south for health or pleasure, and the question of climatic treatment of disease is attracting attention and receiving careful investigation, not only among the medical profession, but in every class of society.

Sick people have but a single wish — that they may get well; and the potential of change of climate from northern inclemency to tropical comfort is so great and is becoming so well-known to-day, that I am persuaded that reliable information concerning our nearest and most accessible neighbors who live beneath the sun, with their surroundings, will be well received by all.

It has ever been a medical opprobrium that most physicians are compelled to order climates for their patients of which they have no personal experience, and whereof their only knowledge is derived from such sources as to make it practically worthless.

"You should make a change, my dear sir," says the puzzled doctor. "Take an ocean voyage, and get out of the bad March winds that are doing you so much harm"

"Willingly, doctor; where shall I go?"

"Well, down South; say to the Windward Islands."

"Yes? To which one, doctor, and how long must I stay? By the way, where is the best hotel, and can I find good physicians? What clothing and money shall I carry? How much will the trip cost? Do they speak English there?" etc., etc. And the doctor answers not, for he does not know. The matter usually ends with search for literature upon the subject, which is comprised in such incorrect books as have been written by rapid tourists, and the showy folders of steamship lines. Neither present any information of sanitary value, and the sick man takes his life with his trunks into a strange and unknown land, where every habit must be changed if he is to gain by the move.

Who is to tell him of this? Perhaps only experience; and that most effective teacher has a way of impressing lessons, now and then, that is funereal.

I am writing this at St. Kitts, the most northern of the group called Leeward Islands, and beside me sits a sea-browned captain who brought his wife and three bright children to the West Indies last fall to avoid the chill winds and rapid weather changes of a New England coast town. They came here and finally found a winter home in the quaint Hollandish island of St. Eustatius, a dozen miles away. Lofty, well drained, swept clean of miasm by constant trade winds — with rain-water to drink that comes from deep rock cisterns covered with conical roofs of stone, and a temperature that changes only three or four degrees in as many months, where could they be better placed?

When they were fairly settled, the mother discovered that the children were with playmates who had sore throat, and made inquiries as to its nature. "Oh, it is nothing serious; we have such sore throats here constantly." A few days later her own contracted the disease, and she called in a physician, who gave no alarm until he saw that they must die, when he pronounced the fatal word — diphtheria. The little ones sleep on that distant islet, and the poor mother cannot forgive the doctor for his lack of skill, or failure of timely warning, or of both.

Across the room sits a prominent merchant of a northern city. He has had constant headache for two weeks following sun heat at Barbados, and paralysis of both lids is slowly closing his eyes. He cannot open them without aid, has double vision, a stumbling gait, and looks ten years older than when he stepped aboard the steamer at New York five weeks ago. He may recover, but it is doubtful.

"Why, doctor," said he, "I had no idea that Barbados sun was so dangerous. No one warned me. If I had only known!"

Case after case comes to mind as memory goes back through the twenty years that I have been wandering among these beautiful islands, where warnings might have saved valuable lives; or given to doomed ones to die at home in place of far away, with only stranger hands to do the last offices.

In making choice of a winter climate for an invalid, while it is essential to know meteorological ranges and have a general idea of soil, water, etc., it is more important to be posted upon such other matters as govern comfort and peace of mind, without which there can be no improvement in health of body. For sunniest skies grow monotonous to idle brains, and balmiest breezes annoying where there is nothing to do. How shall the sick man amuse himself? Are there rides or drives to take? Are there out-of-door games going on? What sort of society is down there? These are important points to all who are not prostrate, and who go to stay some weeks. So they will be carefully considered in our pages.

From the southern point of the Florida peninsula to the northeastern shore of Venezuela, a chain of islands stretches in a graceful curve, occupying some twelve degrees of latitude and five of longitude. From St. Kitts, as Saint Christopher's land is familiarly called, to Trinidad, they are, with the exception of Barbados, mountainous and of volcanic origin; indeed, impressing even careless observers with the belief that they are simply tops of lofty mountains, whose lesser peaks and ranges have been sunk beneath the sea with the continent to which they belonged, by some cataclysm of nature in geologic ages.

From St. Kitts, the Virgin Islands stretch westward, to be joined as neighbors by the Greater Antilles whereof Cuba reigns justly queen. If scientists are correct, the vast Gulf of Mexico was once an inland sea; and where the green waters of the North Atlantic stream sweep in graceful curve, there was a home for nations whose existence is now but matter for conjecture; and the very land that sheltered them, hinted at here and there by ancient writers, may well have been the storied, lost Atlantis. The islands are all intertropical, and differ so little in weather change and rain-fall that the following figures which were given me by Dr. Branch, chief medical officer of St. Kitts and Nevis, may be taken as fairly representing all, with two exceptions to be noted later.

Average annual temperature, 80 degrees F., with a rise in September, the hottest month, to 92°, and a fall in January, the coldest, to 69° in early morning.

Barometric pressure, thirty inches as a mean, from which a fall of one or two tenths is rare and foretells seriously high winds.

STREET IN MACUTO.

Average rain-fall for twenty years, sixty inches; of which the greatest part is deposited in the three rainy months of August, September and October, when it comes in frequent showers rather than steadily. During these months, the trade winds are absent.

Sunny days, with such brilliant skies as northern latitudes are strangers to, are usual during winter and early spring months, except at Martinique, where showers fall at almost any moment, from causes to be explained farther on. At St. Kitts, during the four months ending April 1, 1891, there were but five cloudy days.

When one reads of a steady temperature of 80 degrees, it would seems as if such heat must be uncomfortable; but it is not the case here. There is so much evaporation from skin surface by reason of constant strong winds, that no discomfort is felt unless exposed to direct sun rays, and this must, of course, be avoided.

As I write this, I am sitting in a room where the mercury stands at 72° at 7 A. M., and am actually chilly with the stiff trades blowing my flannel wrap about; and if it should go down to 68°, there would come a general change to heavier clothing, and a furnishing of beds with blankets. I was obliged to put my heavy ulster over me every night at the Hotel des Bains, at Martinique, last March, and at no time was the mercury lower than 70 degrees. And each of my party of five did the same thing.

Therefore, northern ideas of the tropics need reconstructions; and I have never known any one suffer from heat in these islands who exercised ordinary care in avoiding exposure and abstaining from alcoholic drinks. Perhaps as much danger lies therein as in the sun, even at its utmost power. Tippling is such a universal habit, and it is so common to set up cock-tails as a preventive to possible fevers that cautionary advice on this point cannot be made too strong.

Sudden changes of temperature, however slight, must be carefully guarded against. Where every pore is open and

A TROPICAL VERANDAH.

every inch of skin always moist, impact of even a small air current may be followed by a stroke of cold or by what is common among strangers, sharp attacks of muscular rheumatism. From neglect of this fact, I have been laid up three times in the Windward Islands. Natives never sit in a draught, and always wear head covering in doors, in public buildings, hotels, club houses, etc. "Do not remove your hat, sir. You may catch a severe cold, a serious matter here, I assure you." is the kindly advice one hears given to tourists every day in such places.

Drinking-water is everywhere good. In most of the islands it is brought from mountain streams or lakes at great expense; and at Martinique, a constant supply pours through houses and streets from lofty ranges just back of Saint Pierre and Fort de France, in these cities acting as steady and efficient open air sewerage. Except in Jamaica, there has been no idea of impeding sun rays in oxidizing work, and all exposed matters promptly become innocuous and are carried away into the near sea. Zymotic diseases are practically harmless; epidemics of typhoid fever, for instance, being unknown, owing to this excellent sewerage and to an unfailing sweep of pure salt air.

In our party of some fifty persons of all ages, there has not been a single case of trouble of any kind, although nearly every one went ashore daily and drank freely of the different island waters. Nevis, Saint Vincent and a few others, are supplied with rain water, collected in cisterns, carefully protected from contamination.

In most of the towns, food supplies are excellent. Beef and mutton grown in the tropics, lack the tenderness and succulence of northern meat, but they are plentiful and fresh, and their want of quality is condoned by the abundance of fruit, fish, fowl and eggs that is found everywhere; consequently, living is cheap. Two dollars a day is the regular price at all hotels, except the Marine at Barbados and Constant Spring at Jamaica, where American customs and prices obtain without any corresponding gain over native houses; and in large towns, good board may be had for two guineas or about ten dollars a week.

So much for the bright side of our picture. Strangers to these beautiful islands, veritable gems of a summer sea, rarely remain long enough to get the reverse, yet there is one. To many a sea voyage is a sore trial. They see in every curving wave with its glittering foam crest, only a monster that will upset their stomachs and make them generally miserable. They spend long days in uneasy berths, and toss about during longer nights, victims to prostration and repinings. Every strange sound that the engine makes, every blow that a heavier sea than common strikes the rocking ship, every increase of howling song of gale through taut rigging, frightens them anew, and their fate is indeed an unhappy one. In more than twenty years of ocean practice, I have never seen a death attributable to sea sickness, unpleasant as it is, but many cases where long continued nervous prostration followed it; and suggest that a short trial trip precede the tedious voyage hither from New York, made, as it must be at present, in slow ships.

After these years of constant experimenting, I have come to the conclusion that there is no remedy for sea-sickness that is always reliable except solid land. It may not be escaped by the great majority of travelers; it cannot be modified or allayed to any extent by safe means. If any one prefers profound intoxication by drugs or alcohol to temporary disturbance, he may, by producing and maintaining that condition during the entire voyage, avoid it. But the penalty will certainly be exacted and it may prove a heavy one.

When the dismal feeling begins just outside of Sandy Hook, if one will keep on his back in bed or steamer chair, eat often a little liquid food such as beef tea, and drink nothing but iced carbonated water, he will be doing the best possible, and will be all ready for the first shore boat, with an astonishing appetite.

It is a serious matter that transportation to the Windward Islands is not made more pleasant. With the exception of one ship, the *Caribbee*, of the Quebec Line, there is more discomfort and annoyance than is looked for in these days. All return boats are crowded, and it is certain that a better service would be a paying investment. Fares have been very low this season, $108.50 for the round trip, which means five weeks of passage, state-room and meals, with a call at every island, a chance for a run ashore almost daily, a dinner at some quaint hotel, and a look at beautiful scenery.

For those who go to Trinidad or Granada direct, Mr. Christall's fine steamers offer quick passage of six or seven days for $50, and if desired, the tourist may return the other way.

There is a strong probability that this state of affairs will be changed soon, as the Quebec Company is preparing to build a new passenger steamer in this country, which, with the good *Caribbee* and *Bermuda*, will be all that are needed at present.

St. Kitts, British West Indies, March, 1891.

Chapter II.

E left behind the painted buoy
    That tossed outside the harbor's mouth,
And madly danced our hearts with joy,
    As fast we fleeted to the south.
How fresh was every sight and sound
    On open main or winding shore!
We knew the merry world was round,
    And we might sail for evermore.

"Warm broke the breeze against the bow,
    Dry sang the tackle, sang the sail;
The lady's head upon the prow
    Caught the shrill salt and sheered the gale.
The broad seas swelled to meet the keel
    And swept behind; so swift the run
We felt the good ship shake and reel —
    We seemed to sail into the sun."

Careful and thorough consideration should precede decision where to send invalids for climate treatment.

Certain places are favorable for certain diseases, and these may be near together, even in the tropics; but judicious selection is not an easy matter, except the doctor is personally acquainted with the resorts he recommends, or knows some one who is to whom he can refer.

Warm climates by the sea are essentially favorable to nerve rest. Not only does the heated, heavy atmosphere lay its soothing hand upon undue mental or physical work, but examples of *dolce far niente* are seen in every surrounding picture, in every slow lounging movement of those who lend it animation. Then the voyage down to sunny shores is often a veritable cure. Out of sight of land the traveler rests upon the heaving bosom of infinite power, and a brain that is worn out by constant study of details or steady strain of important responsibilities, will find in the journey alone a valuable prescription.

There is total, enforced rest. Reading grows tiresome, even to well people; and such minor incidents as a passing ship or white jet of distant whale-spout, completely fill minds that are wont to be crowded with most important business. Even sea-sickness does its part in destroying memory and thoroughly stimulating the alimentary canal.

A gentleman from Albany said to me this morning at table: "I am astonished at myself. At home I never eat any breakfast except oatmeal and cream, and here I am hungry for more after devouring three substantial steaks, and they don't disagree with me, either."

Any form of nervous prostration or mental tire is usually benefited by these climates. It is best, I believe, to choose a permanent residence in some island where society is good and amusements not unknown, where sea-bathing may be had and a good hotel. In this way, opportunity is afforded for one to grow accustomed to environment, and study customs of other lands, a pursuit always full of interest and profit. He will gain friends able and willing to aid him in search after lost health, and miss the confusion and excitement of shorter visits made upon a mere flying trip, and, best of all, will be afforded time for beneficial results to crystallize, so to speak, into permanent cure.

Mails are infrequent, not arriving oftener than once in ten days or two weeks; and telegrams are such expensive luxuries at $3.00 a word that only sheer need compels their use. All sources of home worry thus cut off, and cold, stormy, northern winter only remembered with pity for such as cannot escape it, convalescence speedily begins. Rest, mental as well as physical, is again possible, and the invalid blesses sound judgment that sent him away.

GOLDEN CACTUS.

Chronic disease of the kidneys is on the list of rare maladies. Case after case within my personal experience has steadily gained in tropical climates, and two of my own were cured thereby, both remaining well after a year north. Perspiration is something astonishing to men whose skins have been dry and harsh for months, and sense of flexible, moist cuticle most agreeable. In one of my cases, the first day at Nassau was marked by restoration of function, followed by rapid gain of flesh, and although sugar did not entirely disappear during the first winter, there was a sense of returning strength and vitality that speedily made drugs unnecessary, and that persisted all the following summer, which was spent climbing about the White Mountains. Briefly, in three winters of tropical sunshine and three summers of bracing mountain air, Mr. D. was cured. For four years now there has been nothing abnormal in his case, and he is again effectively at the head of a great business.

In every case where destruction has not progressed so far as to make even relief of symptoms impossible, I believe that a few seasons in the tropics, with judicious advice while there, will prove a cure. It must be so. Functional rest is the only form of treatment that is inaccessible north, — that nature freely furnishes in these sunny isles; and accompanying this, the valuable tonic, sea-bathing, may be taken every day in the year, in water whose tepid warmth does not over stimulate, and whose purity is guaranteed by three thousand miles of tossing before it comes to land.

There are few more delightful episodes in a sick man's existence than a change from leaden skies, howling winds, and chilling cold of northern winter to constant sunshine, soft trade winds, and delicious daily sea-baths of perpetual summer, with returning sense of capacity for enjoyment. "Life is still worth having," he says, as he gets up at five in the morning, walks down to the beach and enjoys his warm, salt-water bath. There is an exhilaration in matinal hours in the tropics that is contagious. Every thing is awake; turf, trees, and flowers are sparkling with dew; air is cool and sweet, and that vital sense which appropriates its food from nature is completely satisfied.

In all forms of prostration these influences are potent for good, and they are totally inaccessible in winter elsewhere.

The same powerful factors work equally well in what Americans delight in calling nervous exhaustion, when, perhaps, it is the entire system that is depleted of force.

In our party this year were half a dozen professional men, doctors of medicine and divinity, literary men and women, beside several merchants, and, with scarcely an exception, they were "all tired out." One reverend doctor, whose pleasant manners and jovial character made him a general favorite, had been ordered the trip by his physician, in the belief that his exhausted energies would be thereby somewhat restored. But he was mistaken. The clergyman, who had completely and suddenly broken down in nerve, was not to be restored in such a summary manner. He was a sufferer from sea-sickness in a way that was enough, on a rolling ship like ours, to spoil half the voyage; and the rest was far too short for any permanent benefit. As far as it went, or could go, the climate change prescribed was well; but it is always a mistake to send an invalid to sea who is a bad sailor, without a long interval of land rest before the return voyage.

This fact is not generally appreciated, I think, and many who return with but temporary or partial relief from nervous exhaustion, must bethink themselves that nothing more could be expected from such a course.

Causes that have been steadily at work for years, produce effects that are not removable in weeks, and a long, steady, complete rest, with all its environment of quiet, change of air, of scene and food, without excitement or that hardest of work, sightseeing, is required to restore elasticity to the overstrained bow, to permit a reinforcement of nervous force in empty brain and ganglion.

Be it known at once that none of these islands offer, like

European resorts, health in one hand — and a chalice of dissipation foaming full in the other. Here are only eternal summer, delicious fruit, birds that sing and flowers that bloom every day, courteous people and comfortable homes — all at trifling price.

With rare exceptions, streets are empty and people sleeping before nine o'clock. Amusements end with the day, and an hour's quiet chat at club or at home following the usual late dinner, well prepares a nervous person for a calm, restful sleep. Evening parties, except in Jamaica and Trinidad, are very infrequent, and it may be said with truth that natives of the tropics devote their night to sleep.

During the day there are beautiful drives over excellent roads and at moderate prices among scenery so charming that even its novelty in the way of strange plants and flowers is but a small factor of enjoyment; pleasant walks in quaint old towns, among people whose customs are always strange and interesting; visits to shops whose goods are unlike those in our own stores, and very cheap; strolls in early morning to market places where steady rattle of chattering negroes is as odd as are the fruits and vegetables they sell; unending experiments in new dishes at table, which are like a lottery, by no means all prizes, and, above all, the delicious sensation that when breakfast is finished, the day's work is done.

There are local newspapers; but in all my island life I never saw a visitor look at one. Sweet to do nothing indeed, within the tropics, and the hours are too few for the nothing there is to do.

So our patients with tired minds and uncertain brain functions have but to settle quietly down, say good-bye to the ships that brought them hither and regain equilibrium.

A few years ago, a secretary of the treasury gave concern to family and friends, by failing mind and feebleness of usual vigorous judgment. Many cares of state and business had tired out his powerful physique, and with some difficulty he was persuaded to go to Nassau. Here I met him and watched his gain for a few weeks, until he felt so well that he would go back to his post. Warnings were useless, he would go. "Why, doctor," said he, "I sleep perfectly, have a splendid appetite, digest well — in fact, I am *well*. I must get back."

I told him that he was only better; that time bade fair to restore brain tone and make him strong again, but that, while certain nervous symptoms persisted as they did, he was still in danger and ought not to return to work. But remonstrances were useless, and within six months after he had resumed his port-folio, death from cerebral exhaustion claimed another shining victim.

That form of brain congestion that is accompanied with slow, full pulse and general lethargy of function, is promptly benefited by the tropics. It is simply steady heat stimulus that does this, and accelerated skin-action. Surrounded by an atmosphere whose minimum temperature is 68°, and average 78° F., there comes speedy relief to tension of venous circulation in the head. Feet are no longer cold, hands no longer white and flabby; capillaries are full again and brain relieved, and lack of need of heavy clothing to carry around frees from a weighty load. In a short time, pulsation doubles in force, tone and speed, and there is some comfort in living.

A curious circumstance is that smaller doses of hypnotics and narcotics are needed than at the North. I found that a twelfth grain of morphia at Barbados was equal in painkilling power to a quarter grain in New England, and five grains of sodic bromide would induce sleep in a patient accustomed to take twenty-five in Boston. Inquiry among druggists showed that their average doses of these drugs prescribed was much smaller than ours. This condition is probably caused by lack of interfering nervous excitement and greater general quiet.

Fat people grow thinner here. One lady, who weighed over two hundred when she arrived at Port of Spain, left there, after three months, happy in possession of a hundred and forty pounds and greatly increased comfort. For this pleasant result her constant profuse perspiration and a diet largely of fruit, together with daily carriage exercise, were responsible. All these scarcely attainable elsewhere, certainly not North in winter time.

Thin people, whose lankness is due to dyspepsia, find themselves eating and comfortably caring for an amount of food that would have been impossible at home, and gain weight. In seven days at Martinique, I gained five pounds.

Perhaps the most brilliant results of heat in climate cure are seen in that puzzling form of functional nervous disorder known as neurasthenia. At its worst, there are few diseases whose unfortunate possessor is regarded with more dread by his physician. There is so little to do, and the patient demands so much! Well, doctor, if you can persuade him to take the West Indian voyage, you will probably have one patient less when spring comes. Sea-sickness and fidgets are mortal enemies, and active vomiting leaves small time for querulous complaints. By the time St. Kitts is reached, the patient is ready to go ashore and enjoy novel sights as well as any one, and the entire lack of sympathy for fancied disease that strangers exhibit is a better cure

NIGHT WORK IN A SUGAR MILL.

than strychnine or steel. Then, whatever may have been the cause of trouble, it is gone. New surroundings, strange sights, and an atmosphere without any sharp points in it combine to keep the mind busy and soothe uneasy nerves; so that the neurastheniac finds himself wondering, some fine morning, that he has forgotten to complain.

I am assuming in this statement that there is no organic complication. When there is, I give the disease another name.

In all derangements of the heart this climate is invaluable. In valvular diseases and fatty degeneration great comfort follows the change. Symptoms are greatly ameliorated or disappear, and the amount of comfort obtained, almost at once, is striking. A single case in point may be cited, and might be added to by others.

An army surgeon contracted acute rheumatism in 1861, from exposure. The attack lasted six weeks, with frequent change of location, and was followed by heart disease, from which an apparent recovery was made, and nothing thought further of the matter. During the battle of Antietam, eighteen months later, he was struck on the chest by a spent piece of shell, which nearly prostrated him, and that also passed unnoticed. Not until 1876, fourteen years later, did serious symptoms occur, which then assumed such proportions that a consultation was ordered, and examination by three of the leading chest specialists in the country revealed an organic change, and they agreed that life must be brief; one of them, Prof. Loomis, giving two weeks as the probable extent.

But the doctor was plucky; and knowing, from experience, the good effect of warm climates in similar cases, started promptly for Cuba, whence he returned after two months, in apparently sound health. All constitutional signs had disappeared, and a second examination gave greatly decreased murmur, nearly normal capacity for running and climbing, and normal muscular strength.

This state continued until winter came again, when the old weak feelings, pain over heart and down left arm, and inability to mount stairs, all returned. This time he did not wait for any consultation, but started at once for sunny lands, whence he again returned in early spring, well.

Briefly, these journeys have been repeated every winter since, and my friend is in the enjoyment of excellent health, immense capacity for work and enjoyment, and the two weeks lease of life has expanded to fourteen years, with fair prospects for fourteen more, if cold be avoided.

In thus sketching briefly some cases that are benefited by a visit to the tropics, I by no means present that climate as a panacea. Certain maladies get well there, others grow rapidly worse; and, in the next chapter, it is my purpose to speak of the latter — to warn against going south, as so far I have advised it.

MARTINIQUE, W. I., March, 1891.

Chapter III.

SUNNY climes, equal temperature of torrid heat, beautiful scenery, and all magic of change, cannot always prolong life.

It is especially important, in choosing a locality for a sick man for whom change is deemed advisable, to consider carefully what effect certain climates have upon certain classes of disease, and to learn as accurately as may be, the environment to which he will be subjected when once there.

I use the word subjected because I mean it. It is a serious matter for any one who is unaccustomed to travel, indeed for almost every one, to pull up stakes that have been driven deep and long, and start; so serious that most who go must stay for a time, if they like it or not.

More than once, in fact more times than I can now remember, I have seen sick people banished from home, friends, and the delights of their own fireside, without the smallest chance of permanent improvement following the change, either for the purpose of relieving some tired doctor of an incurable patient, or to gratify the wishes of the person himself.

It is indeed a pitiful sight when one of these poor fellows steps ashore at Nassau or Barbados, with every sign of incurable consumption in his emaciated form and lustreless eyes, and to think that the only probable way in which he may see his native land again is by vision from the next world.

IN THE SQUARE, IN ST. KITTS.

The other day I stopped such a man as this in the street at St. Kitts. "Where do you come from," asked I. "From Philadelphia," he answered "Yes? Do you come out here for your health?" (an unnecessary question, by the way). "Yes, by the advice of my doctor," (naming a well-known specialist of that city). "Had your doctor ever been in the West Indies, do you know?" "I don't think he had, sir, because when we were talking about the islands, and I wanted to know which one would be best for my peculiar condition, he answered: 'It does not make any difference, they are all just alike, go to which one you choose and make yourself comfortable.' So here I am, and so far as I can see, without much chance of either making myself or being made comfortable, in this island, at least."

"Do you know, sir," he continued, "if any of the other islands are better than this for a man whose lungs are half gone?"

"Why, yes," I replied, "this is probably the worst of all, for here there are neither hotels nor any means of passing away time excepting praying to the good Lord to let you live long enough to get back home again. You should have gone to Barbados, where the air is much dryer than here; where there is a choice of three or four hotels, and where there is plenty to occupy your time, even if you should want a change of occupation every day."

"Well," he said, "that's all these doctors know about things. If mine had told me what you tell me now, I might have been comfortably settled in Barbados by this time, instead of looking around St. Kitts for something to eat."

"How long have you been here?" I asked.

"A week to-day."

"Are you feeling better, and does the air agree with you? Do you cough less, and is your appetite better?" were some of the questions I asked this poor fellow, in the interests of sick men to come after.

"I think," was the reply, "that I do cough less; but then the weather at home, when I left, was simply awful, and the perfection of climate here is such a change that one must be well-nigh dead not to gain by it; but I find that the constant perspiration brought on by the temperature, even without the smallest exertion, and which continues night and day, is making me sensibly weaker, and I fear that I have not done right in coming away from home at all."

I could not find it in my heart to tell the poor fellow that I thoroughly agreed with him. I have not heard since what became of him, but have no hesitation in saying that it was a serious mistake to send a case of consumption in any form or at any stage, except perhaps the very first of bronchial irritation, to these islands of the south; one reason being that the temperature, an absolutely permanent one for certain seasons of the year, is always sufficiently high to produce perspiration, which in a well person, or one affected by certain nervous diseases, is a good thing, but which in a consumptive weakens the patient.

In all my twenty years' experience among the tropics, I have never seen a case of advanced tubercular disease improved to any extent or in any permanent way by a residence therein, temporary or otherwise. On the contrary, it has been my sad lot to aid in preparing for the grave more than one lonely friend who had left all that life holds dear behind, in order that he might seek a futile chance for life; and I cannot say in too strong words, nor with too emphatic accents, that it is worse than useless to send consumptives to these islands.

I do not, in this statement, include such diseases of the throat as are catarrhal, irritative, or depend for continuance upon malignant northern winters. On the contrary, all these forms are rapidly improved, and in many cases permanently cured by the change.

Loss of voice, especially dependent upon catarrhal inflammation of the larynx or chords, disappears like magic. Rough accents soften down beneath the influence of the warm salt air and continuous moisture, and the change seems incredible to the sufferer.

Forms of cough that are dependent upon throat irritation, whether the same be nervous or not, do not last in this climate more than twenty-four hours; in fact, they are gone so quickly that it is a matter of wonder with the patient when they disappear, and he asks himself if he was not mistaken in supposing he had any.

It is, therefore, my deliberate opinion that of the two classes of disease called consumption in the north, one being true tuberculosis and the other functional or nervous throat disease, the first has no business in any tropical climate, but should be sent inland to some place like Colorado. The second does well here if sufficient time be given to consummate the cure that a flying trip only gives an opportunity to have commenced.

Tropical islands are bad places for rheumatism; the same constant moisture that plays so large a part in curing nervous difficulties produces and intensifies all forms of rheumatic inflammation. It is a common disease. I cannot state the exact percentage, but from the number of natives that I have seen complaining of it, I am satisfied that it is a staple malady.

Probably a larger percentage of these cases are muscular than with us, for the reason that there are no sharp changes of temperature to intensify a passing irritation into acute disease; but they are sufficiently annoying. Three times have I been prostrate with lumbago which was difficult to be rid of, and in each case it followed a seemingly trifling cause.

The skin is constantly in a state of high activity; at no time, night or day it is dry, and the result of even a slight breeze striking this wet body is to lower its temperature a little. It is but a trifle, probably not felt at all, or, if felt, but eagerly welcomed as a pleasant relief from previous heat.

You do not even draw the loose wrap over your evening dress, or take the trouble to cover bare shoulders with more than a lace veil, but when next morning comes, there is an acute attack of lumbago to face. You are tied to your bed as if every muscle when put in motion was a red-hot bundle of wires. Nothing but absolute quiet can prevent acute agony, and this is as hard to cure in the tropics as it is here. It can, however. be totally avoided, as I have learned by experience during the last three years, by wearing pure woolen under-clothing of medium weight next the skin, and changing it as often as it gets wet with perspiration. The latter is as important a precaution as the former, for wet flannel is not in any degree an improvement over dry cotton.

Diseases of the eyes are not uncommon in these islands, which are as a rule composed partly of coral, some of them entirely so; and the intense whiteness of streets, buildings and beaches, in full glare of vertical sun, is bad treatment for those that come from abroad.

It is necessary to protect these sensitive organs everywhere in the tropics, by shading them from the sun with umbrellas whose lining is green, or by constantly wearing blue or smoked goggles. Neglect to heed this advice will be almost sure to be followed by some form of temporary blindness. If anything of this kind should occur, a mild astringent eye lotion with seclusion from the sun for a day or two, will be curative. If there is any tendency to inflammatory conditions of the eye, the tourist must be thoroughly impressed with the necessity of great additional care when he goes to the islands.

Although contagious diseases are not usual in the islands, they still exist, modified in a large degree by the almost perfect drainage that is common everywhere, by a profusion of pure water, a comparative disuse of meat as a diet, and constant life in the open air.

Derangements of the digestive organs are only common here among strangers, who persist in bringing to the islands northern appetites, and in demanding that they be supplied by northern food. They eat as much in Martinique as they do in New York, and sit at the table of the hotel wondering at the quantity of fruit and vegetables devoured by those to the manner born.

It must be remembered that the tropics furnish heat sufficient to satisfy the body when the inner fires are fed with fuel that burns slowly, and abstain from loading the system with anything requiring much effort to get rid of. One is not often comfortable until the blood is thinned down from its sluggish northern flow, and only then begins to feel well when to the thinness is added a perceptible acidity.

It is my habit as soon as I arrive in the tropics, to begin eating fruit in great profusion, both at the early morning meal and through the hours of the forenoon, abstaining entirely from meat. When I have taken so much as to produce a continuous sour taste in the mouth, and a feeling as if the teeth were on edge every time an acid touches them. I restrict myself to two oranges and a tumbler of cocoanut milk in the early morning, eating meat with great care, living chiefly on vegetables and fish. In this way I avoid altogether dyspeptic derangements, and am able in a few days to stand the heat and prolonged exertion as well as the natives.

I think strangers would do well to follow my example in this respect, at least to some extent.

Should indigestion or dyspepsia follow the injudicious use of meat, it is much better to apply to one of the thoroughly qualified native physicians than to take drugs from the pocket-case that invariably accompanies travelers.

One of the ladies of my party carried two medicine cases, either of which contained a greater variety and better selection of drugs than the ship's chest, and when we returned, both were empty.

In almost every one of the islands there are native remedies unknown in the United States, that are much better fitted for those localities than imported ones, and it is therefore preferable to have a native doctor.

GUADELOUPE, W. I., March, 1891.

Chapter IV.

I HAD intended, in closing my last chapter, to have spoken a few words upon the subject of clothing to be worn in the tropics and the amount of baggage to be taken.

In the first place, voyagers may place themselves entirely at ease in respect to customhouse authorities. All manner of courtesy is shown to tourists, and trunks or bags of any kind are rarely opened in the islands, officers going through the formula of chalking with the utmost rapidity and a pleasant smile.

This rule does not hold good on the Spanish Main, nor in any country in South America. Those who contemplate a visit to the sister continent must take the few succeeding paragraphs as applying to the islands only.

In fact, at Martinique, the time occupied in passing my two trunks and two cameras was inside of sixty seconds; none of the packages were opened, and, with a courteous smile, the inspector said: "We never trouble the baggage of tourists, for there is no danger of their bringing anything here to cheat customs." And the same being the case at all the other islands, there is no possible need to abstain from carrying as many trunks as one wishes. On board ship they are swung down into the hold, no extra charge is made for their transportation, and, arriving at one or the other central points aimed at, a depot may be readily established, and small baggage taken thence in any direction.

It is difficult to estimate the value of one's own clothes when away from home. There is a sentiment of placid content in the mind of the traveler who has all the changes that he wants, that goes far to make him happy, while the one who has come away with a couple of suits only, soon finds that he has made a mistake.

It is not here as in Europe, where every pound of baggage must be paid for extra, at a rate that speedily makes one's necessaries cost more to transport than himself.

All due deference is paid to luggage in the British islands, and it is expected of the transportation lines that they should carry everything free.

It is a common thing to see a great boat-load of trunks going off on board a steamer of the Royal Mail, and to be told that these belong to a single passenger, when a casual observation would have convinced a looker-on that they were the entire baggage supply from a hotel. It is totally unnecessary to economize in this direction.

Under no circumstances, and I take the liberty to repeat this admonition, should anything but woolen underclothing be worn next the skin, and, bearing in mind the fact that West India washerwomen laundry their clothes by laying them on one rock and hammering them with another, it is as well to carry a supply sufficient for the trip, as I always do, or to purchase garments upon arriving, and to present them in fee-simple to the laundress who comes to collect soiled linen.

The same rule holds good with gentlemen's flannels. There is no place in the West Indies where they can be cleansed as at home, and for this reason fancy tennis and yachting flannels are rarely seen among the natives, who content themselves with plain suits of blue or gray. Garments of white linen are rarely worn. It is a mistake to suppose that they are cooler. The expense of washing and repairing is something enormous, they are quickly soiled, and not easily replaced.

Ladies in this climate rarely wear white, except at evening parties, or for morning wraps.

One begins by being surprised at the heavy clothing people wear down here, and ends by putting on something of the same kind with exceeding joy, after an attack of lumbago caught by exposure to currents of air.

Serviceable flannel dresses for the day, cashmere gowns for breakfast, woolen or silk dresses for dinner, are what are needed. These, it is true, may be procured at a very reasonable price from native dressmakers, but they will rarely be satisfactory to the wearer anywhere away from the town where they are bought. It is better to take all that sort of thing along.

The same with shoes. The feet of the women of these countries are larger, on an average, than those of our own, and the ladies of my party found it a practical impossibility to re-shoe themselves when their own boots had given out. Carry therefore plenty of boots.

In the French islands there are milliners who get up astonishing head-gear, some of the efforts made in Martinique being, as I was assured by a fair dame of our party, equal to anything she had seen in New York.

Do not take the trouble to bring umbrellas or sunshades. They may be purchased here in infinite variety, and at a price far below those at home. Everybody carries an umbrella, either for sun or rain, and no one is disappointed in finding a use for them.

With this dissertation on the clothes that one has to wear

and needs to carry, we will fancy the long and tedious voyage at an end, and the islands of Saba and St. Eustatius in sight.

Over Little Saba, often called "Napoleon's Cocked Hat," from its singular resemblance to that article of apparel, hung soft fleecy clouds, which presently saluted us with sharp rain gusts and in a moment the sun shone out bright again.

No one seemed to know much about these places, and I was glad, a little later, to get hold of a book about them, and meet a gentleman who had recently been there.

Saba's little colony of two thousand or more poor negroes live like sea-birds in an eyrie, away up on the volcanic peak that climbs a thousand feet farther toward the sky. There they spend their idle lives, raising a few vegetables, and occasionally building a boat for fishing purposes.

Once in a way, there is diversion afforded them, for their mountain home has a habit of occasionally exploding; the last eruption, in 1869, having been severe enough to shake up the people of St. Thomas, fifty miles away, in an energetic manner, but without making any particular impression upon their own minds.

I heard also that this gentleman had been exported from Holland to Saba to get well of chronic bronchitis, and that he preferred the bronchitis to the cure.

As there is neither an hotel nor a boarding-house, nor much of anything else on the island, there is little to buy, and it is useless for tourists' purposes.

Only a little way, however, across a sea of absolutely tranquil blue, the mountain peaks of St. Kitts assume form against the sky. Above the rugged cliffs of the Soufrière dark clouds of smoke hung thick, with here and there a vision of flame, as the crater below talked to us.

From beneath the clouds to the very water's edge stretched down the fields of sugar-cane in softest, sweetest tints of living green, divided into fields by mere difference of color. Of all rapid thorough cures for sea-sickness commend me to pictures like these. Not one of the growlers who had been so troublesome all the way out, remained; every one was joyful, well and happy, and exclamations of delight were heard on every hand, with expressions of thankfulness that they had come.

Along the sloping hill-side, excellent roads shone white among the green. Here and there tall chimneys marked sugar estates, and deep gullies in mountain sides told of furious floods in rainy times.

At last we came in sight of Basseterre, chief town and capital of the island, whose population is some thirty thousand souls, the island, not the city. Like all tropical towns, it is prettiest from the sea, if I except the well-kept public square and the garden around the church, which are singularly attractive to eyes dimmed to out-door beauties by a long northern winter.

There, in February, Marechal Niel and Jacqueminot roses were blooming in open air in serene unconsciousness of frost and snow that was good to see, and in the park avenues, tall palms with graceful waving fronds of deepest green, and long lines of mango-trees, just then in full bloom, gave no hint of winter near.

The temperature was simply perfect; neither too hot nor too cold. It was a fitting accompaniment to the natural graces of the beautiful island we were on.

The most thorough searcher for curios failed to find anything to buy, with the exception of a few specimens of tropical fruits, and the shops, to people who had lately left

PUBLIC FOUNTAIN, ST. KITTS.

Broadway, were scarcely worth mentioning; but to our sea-weary passengers it was Eden, and their ecstasies over the beautiful flowers and trees recalled some early experiences of my own when the tropics were new to me too.

Hotels there are none worthy of mention; but the government has made an offer of seven thousand pounds sterling to build one, and will purchase a suitable tract of land within a short time. For the present, visitors who remain over a steamer are made fairly comfortable at Mrs. Syder's. I spent a week in her care, and found little to complain of except irregularity of meal hours; but no one cares to be regular in time matters there. And a visitor is sure to be entertained so hospitably away from his inn that meals are not of as much consequence as if he were living in a hotel at home.

There is an excellent hospital, named for a former governor, Cunningham. It has one hundred and thirty beds, of which fifty are surgical, with well-ventilated, cleanly wards, furnished with neat iron bedsteads, and there is every evidence in and about it of careful and attentive supervision and skilful medical service.

With just a few words more we will take leave of St. Kitts. It has the honor of being the mother colony of the British West Indies, having been settled by Sir Thomas Warner in 1623.

Excellent water is brought from the hills five miles away, and there is plenty of it. There are beautiful drives, and equally attractive rides, the most popular being the drive and climb up Monkey Hill, a sharp elevation on the south end of the island, where was once a strong fortification, whose ruins now are held by a garrison of apes.

No finer tropical scenery can be found in any of the islands.

than is afforded by a drive from Basseterre across to the north coast and along to the little village of Cayon, six or seven miles each way. The proper carriage fare is $7.00 for two horses and four seats, or $5.00 for one horse and two seats, for this trip.

Nevis goes fairly with St. Kitts, from which it is separated by a narrow arm of the sea, scarcely a mile wide. One should not leave St. Kitts without a visit to Nevis; for, beside the most wonderful hot spring and bath in the Windward Islands, there are the ruins of a once magnificent hotel, the birthplace of Alexander Hamilton, and a quaint old church in which I found the following record: "Married, March 17, 1783, Horatio Nelson, Esq., Captain of His Majesty's Ship *Boreas*, and Frances Nesbitt, widow."

Besides all this, the visiting American, if he is as fortunate as I was, will meet cordial hospitality from Dr. Huggins and his charming Yankee wife.

So Nevis should by no means be neglected.

St. Kitts, February, 1891.

Chapter V.

ON leaving St. Kitts, a gentleman sitting by my side remarked (we were then on our return trip from Trinidad): "If somebody who had taken the trouble to write articles about these places had only told us when we were here before that the very best green turtle dinner that the islands can afford is furnished by the proprietor of the American Hotel at Antigua, upon receipt of a telegram to that effect from here, my opinion is that everybody would be very glad to take it in." So, upon this suggestion I put it down. It is one night's trip across an arm of the sea to Antigua, and the ship dropped anchor early in the morning, at the nearest point to the picturesque town of St. Johns that lay spreading out at the foot of a hill three or four miles away.

From our anchorage, Mr. Ellery, the courteous harbor master, took us in his steam launch.

There are as attractions in the city of St. Johns, the prettiest work in black and red seeds that I ever saw, specimens of petrified tropical woods from a valley a little way inland, called the "Valley of Petrifactions," and a public library containing several thousand volumes, large school maps of the island with a collection of natural curiosities which would be of some use if they were labeled.

Also there is a beautiful view from the upper windows of a fine cathedral.

The drives about the island are not especially interesting, for it is devoid of striking contrasts of scenery, but they are of quiet beauty, and the air is heavy with the scent that makes even tolerable roads enjoyable. If there is time, a drive should be taken to English Harbor, across the island, where there is a navy-yard of the style of 200 years ago. where British men-of-war came to refit after their fierce battles with the French in these waters. Looking down from the verandah of Clarence House, the massive building brought out from England for William IV. when commanding the fleet as Duke of Clarence, the picture is a charming one. The walls of the house are nine feet thick, insuring coolness and a safe foundation when hurricanes come. A hundred feet below, the buildings and docks of the arsenal, kept in immediate readiness for use, look like shining yellow toy houses, and the sea around them like Norwegian fiords. Carriages for the drive may be had for ten dollars, to carry four, and half a day is necessary. For the rest of the description of this island, my friend Dr. Gardiner has consented to provide my readers with one, which is as much better than mine as might be expected from an old resident. Listen to him.

"Antigua is situated in the Caribbean Sea, between 17° 2' and 17° 3' north latitude, and between 61° 44' and 61° 58' west longitude ; of a rough circular figure, twenty miles long, fifty-four in circumference, and much indented by creeks and bays.

"Although properly classed with the Calcareous Islands, not half of its strata come under that description, while the remainder consists of trap rocks and curious marine and fresh water deposits, furnishing the amateur geologist with many interesting facts and problems.

"The island is flat, with the exception of the southwestern division which is hilly. Some of these mountains rise with conical summits to the height of one thousand feet; others, of the same elevation, are more rounded and less precipitous, affording a good soil for sugar-cane. They are intersected by beautifully romantic valleys, and the abrupt sides of the mountains are clothed with the verdant foliage of a great variety of herbs and twining shrubs.

"St. Johns, the capital, is on the northwest coast of the island, and presents on the approach to the harbor a very picturesque appearance, from the beauty of its situation and generally neat aspect. It is a well laid out city, the principal streets are wide, crossed by others at right angles, and the town extends from east to west, having a gentle declivity towards the harbor, the highest point being about forty feet above the level of the sea. The water supply is ample, and is conducted by iron pipes into every street of the city.

"The Board of Health is vigilant, and the hygienic condition of the town is very good; in fact, the members of the Board pride themselves in saying that no other town in the West Indies can compare with St. Johns from a sanitary point of view.

"Climate: — The weight and temperature of the atmosphere vary but little throughout the year, and especially is this so during the months of January, February and March, when the fanning trade wind holds its steady course, infusing health and vigor into every living creature. The mean temperature of the year is 78° F.; the maximum, 89° F. During January this year the highest temperature registered was 80° F.; the lowest, 74° F.; average being 76° F. During February the highest was 80° F.; lowest, 74° F.; average, 78° F. During March the highest was 88° F.; lowest, 74° F; average, 80° F. The above figures were taken at 9 A. M. and 4 P. M each day, but during the cloud-

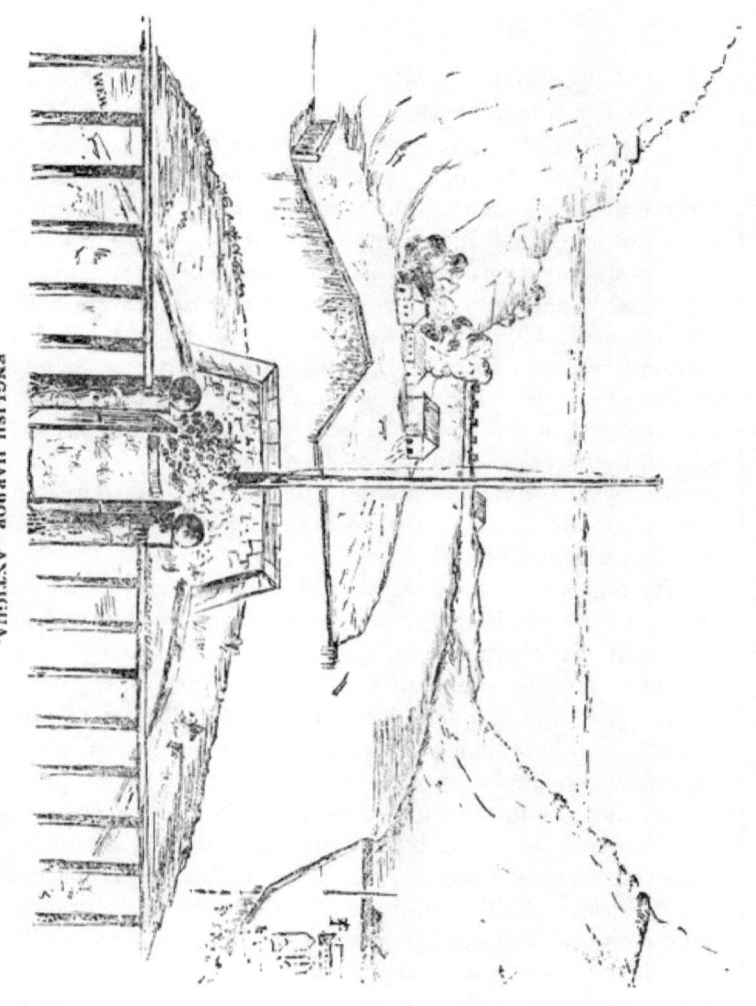

ENGLISH HARBOR, ANTIGUA.

less moonlight nights at this period of the year the mercury occasionally falls to 66° F.

"The rainfall for January this year was 5' 21"; for February, 1' 00"; for March, 2' 51". In comparing the rainfall for these months during the last ten years, I find that we have had more than the average amount this year.

"Accommodations:—At present we have one comfortable hotel, capable of putting up from twelve to eighteen visitors, at a cost of thirty-five dollars a month; but there are private boarding-houses where board and lodging can be had at a cheaper rate. I may mention that the members of the Legislative Council are at present considering the advisability of granting a subsidy of seven hundred pounds per annum, with the view of establishing a first-class hotel on American principles, so as to perfect as far as possible the island as a health resort.

"As regards luxuries for the table we are very well off here. For example, ice at one penny per pound; oysters at one penny per dozen; turtle eggs and green turtle for a few shillings; venison seven pence per pound; land crabs, guinea fowls and a large and varied supply of fish. Tropical fruits abound, Antigua being famed far and wide for its pineapples, which can be purchased for a few cents each.

"By way of amusements we have a well-stocked library, an abundance of tennis courts, cricket, billiards, shooting, Cinderella dances, concerts, etc. The sea bathing is charming, the water of a beautiful blue color, never too cold, just sufficient to enliven and invigorate, and can be enjoyed by all.

"The inhabitants are hospitable, and from being the seat of government for the Leeward Islands, the society can compare favorably with the surrounding islands. We have two clubs, where strangers may be introduced and pleasant evenings spent.

"Business men, nervous and melancholic from over-work and worry, will find a trip to Antigua healthful, pleasant and agreeable, returning home in good spirits, refreshed and invigorated.

"From the above statistics it will be seen that there are no deaths from fevers. Visitors need not be afraid of con-

The Point Antigua

tracting any malarial taint, which, when it is prevalent in the autumn, is of a mild type. An epidemic of yellow fever has not been known here for over twenty years.

PETER GARDINER, C. M., M. D."

In addition to what my friend Dr. Gardiner has said of the hotel accommodations at Antigua, I must put in another word for the excellent green turtle dinners that are served at the American Hotel at short notice, and remind my readers of

UNDER THE SOUTHERN CROSS.

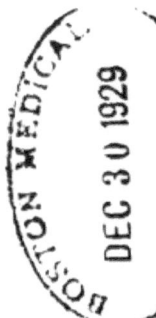

at I said in a previous paragraph about cabling over from Kitts at the landlord's expense, to have one of them ready when the ship gets in.

There are the usual stories about Captain Kidd, going about Antigua, and one of our passengers picked up a fine specimen of a pine-tree shilling for a few pence, which he afterwards sold for thirty-five dollars, which, of course, came from the pirate's hoard.

About the lovely bay, which is full of pretty islets, there is good fishing and sailing for those who like the water, and, take it altogether, it seems to me that a traveler might do far worse than to settle down for a couple of winter months in St. Johns.

Of the island of Dominica there is more to be said from the tourist's point of view than from that of a sanitarian. Some four hundred years ago when Columbus sighted the lofty peaks of Roseau, it chanced to be Sunday, and the admiral, with his usual piety, named it Dominica, Sunday Land.

Its capital town is anything but interesting from an artistic or comfortable point of view. Mrs. Ogilvy has a very fair inn, however, and after ten days with her, I can commend her hostelry to any one who is not too dependent upon luxuries. It is clean, service fair, and food sufficient, and the charges are $2.00 per diem. But the inhabitants, with generous hospitality, are always ready to find comfortable resting-places for those who come to stay among them.

The chief annoyance to sleepy travelers in Dominica is the number of noisy curs that infest the streets, and howl with steady energy every hour of the otherwise restful night. I know a gentleman resident in Roseau, who keeps a box full of rocks of convenient size in his bed-room, and spends part of almost every night throwing them at dogs.

But if the town is not attractive, the island itself is very much the reverse, for of all the scenery that the West Indies boasts, whether of mountain gorge, deep, dim, verdure-clad valley, or of precipitous orchid-clad mountain side, there are no better examples than may be found in beautiful Dominica. One cannot obtain even a slight idea of its charm without going at least as far up the hills as the famous fall of the boiling springs, and as this involves an entire day, there are few of the tourists by any of the present lines who have an opportunity to study it. Then, too, on the other side of the island from the town of Roseau, there is a tribe of ancient Caribs, or of their descendants, who retain in that inaccessible spot the customs, costumes and manners of the native lords of the soil. But there are twenty-five miles of virgin forest, glades and mountain gorges to traverse to reach them, and one must camp out one night on the way, as there are no places to stop, and as this requires a fit-out of servants, animals and tents, there are not many who venture upon the expedition.

But I cannot leave Dominica without speaking of the well-known boiling springs to which we did go, and which I carefully examined.

Leaving town early in the morning, accompanied by a guide, I rode out of the city and set my face toward the distant mountain. Beyond a shallow stream that wound across the path, where darkey women were washing clothes between two rocks, the road plunges into a plantation of lime trees, whose golden fruit hung thick overhead among the dark, waxy leaves, or rolled in profusion among the horses' feet, till we came to the factory where the juices are squeezed out, boiled down and shipped to England to be bottled. A little later on, we began the steep ascent upon a road that wound steadily upward beside a mountain stream, in the cool shade of overhanging cliffs, and such glorious luxuriance of tropical foliage as is rarely found even in these islands. There were clusters of tree ferns, sixty or one hundred feet high, with trunks as thick as one's body, and leaves ten feet long, each one as delicately cut as the little fronds that we find in dark valleys of our own mountains. What the names were of other trees around us, each one of which was wound with parasitic vines, loaded with air plants of every kind, we had no means of ascertaining, for none of us were botanists.

We halted at mid-day for a little lunch at a point where the barometer measured twenty-two hundred feet elevation. At this place was a sugar estate called "Wotten Waven," that belonged to the American consul, Mr. Stedman. After luncheon we kept on a little way until in a ravine we heard the jerky puffs of steam like a high pressure engine, and began to smell the sulphur of the boiling springs. In the bed of the stream made by the spring water, there was a circular depression some six feet across, in which thick blue mud was seething and boiling in the fiercest way. Little cones from the mud burst with mimic explosion, and gave place to open craters which in turn soon became cones. Beneath the ledge on which I sat to sketch, there was rumbling and trembling as of a steam boiler close below with the safety valve tied down. It soon grew so hot that I was glad to get up, and a thermometer bulb, pressed into the spot I had vacated, marked one hundred and sixty degrees.

A little farther on was the main spring about fifteen feet across, over which, even in that hot air, were clouds of steam. I went to the edge of the water with considerable caution, and found its temperature two hundred and eight degrees. In a moment there came an eruption, and jets of boiling water from every part of the surface were thrown up at least twenty feet in the air; then an interval of quiet of six minutes, and another eruption, and the guide said that this was the usual condition of things. Although the air was loaded with the scent of sulphuretted hydrogen, I found no evidence of free sulphur to any extent. Stones and limbs of trees in the water course showed no deposit, and a silver coin, held a few minutes in the stream, was not discolored. Probably the metal was vaporized by the intense heat of the spring.

This excursion may readily be taken in the short time that the steamer remains in port, and is by no means too far for a pedestrian of fair powers to walk. Ponies may be hired for $1.50 each and visitors will find a black man named Cockroach the most reliable person to deal with in obtaining them.

Farther on in the depths of these virgin forests, there is a great boiling lake which has been visited by very few white men. My friend Ober, author of "Camps in the Carribees," is the only one, as far as I know, who has made any study of it, and I commend a trip to the Boiling Lake of Dominica as worthy the attention of tourists.

For curiosities, there are pretty stuffed humming-birds, at sixpence apiece; immense Hercules or saw beetles with peculiar lower mandible, at a shilling, and Carib baskets, made of some part of the palm tree, in all sizes, and prices, which will stand rain or hold water, and make famous travelling baskets.

The following interesting sketch was sent me by Dr. Nichols, chief medical officer, who has been a resident for twenty years and is acknowledged authority.

"The parallel of 15° 17' 27" N. latitude, and the meridian of 61° 23' 32" W. longitude, pass through Roseau, the capital of Dominica, the loveliest, the most interesting, but one of the least known islands of the New World.

At the present day one of the most interesting facts in connection with Dominica, is the presence of some hundreds of its original inhabitants; but these remnants of an ancient people retain nothing of their fierceness of by-gone times, for they are now gentle in demeanor and timid in nature, and are rarely seen away from the land allotted to them by the government, and called by the people the Indian Country. They retain, however, their skill in hunting, and they will even now venture out fishing in a sea, the roughness of which would scare the best boatman of the windward coast.

The deep sea soundings, made in the U. S. steamer *Blake*, under the superintendence of Professor Alexander Agassiz and Commander Bartlett, U. S. N., show that Dominica was at one time the southern extremity of a gigantic triangular-shaped island, the base of which extended from Sombrero to within a short distance of Santa Cruz. The shores of this island are submerged 500 feet below the level of the sea and its principal mountain ranges are now the islands of Dominica, Guadeloupe, Montserrat, Antigua, St. Christopher, Nevis, Barbuda, St. Martin, and Anguilla. Professor Agassiz and Captain Bartlett, by their 1,000 feet soundings, take us still further back into pre-historic time, and show that Dominica was countless years ago the centre of a long promontory extending from the mainland of South America, which then included Trinidad, Tobago, and Grenada, to within a spot near to the Virgin Islands.

In some districts volcanic action is still going on, and thermal springs exist in several localities. The largest extinct volcano, about 2,000 feet above the level of the sea and eight miles N. E. of Roseau, is situated in a depression of the central range of mountains which runs through the length of the island like a backbone, and it contains a crater lake of about a mile and a half in circumference. The depth of the lake averages sixty feet, and the water is of varying temperature, warm springs bubbling from below to mingle with the upper stratum of cool water which results from the surface drainage of the surrounding mountain side. The lake is now the source of the chief tributary of the Roseau River, and at the head of the Roseau Valley the stream tumbles over a precipice 150 feet in height, and forms one of the two magnificent Roseau water-falls.

The boiling lake lies to the northeast of the largest and less active *soufrière*, from which it is separated by a sloping ridge, composed for the most part of scoria and ash. It is a body of slate-colored water enclosed in an ovoid crater, with almost perpendicular sides averaging 60 feet in height. At its northwest extremity a small stream of cold water finds its way to the lake, and the outlet is at the eastern end through a break in the sides of the crater, but the volume of water leaving the lake is much larger than that of the stream flowing into it. The hot water charged with sulphur and decomposed rock, which flows from the lake, forms one of the head springs of the Point Mulatre River, a powerful torrent which even at the sea-side frequently bears evidence of its parentage. The Boiling Lake is about two hundred yards in length, by more than half the same amount in breadth. It is at times quiescent, but on most occasions when it has been visited, the water has been in a state of ebullition, and the crater has been filled with clouds of steam and sulphurous vapors given off from its surface. So dense, indeed, are these white clouds, that only when a breeze blows them aside can the lake be seen for a moment from the edge of the water. The point of ebullition is not in the centre, but toward the southeastern extremity; the water is here elevated like a mound several feet above the general surface, and the force of the ebullition causes a violent agitation of the whole body of the lake. The sulphurous gases have exerted a solvent effect on the light colored rocks forming the crater, for they are soft, and they may easily be made to crumble away by the exertion of a little force. The slate-colored water of the lake, which is dense with sulphur and decomposed rock, has at times a circular movement, and the stones and rocks at the margin of the water are coated with pure sulphur.

The Boiling Lake of Dominica is a most wonderful phenomenon, and when seen it strikes the beholder with awe. In the first published account of the lake the discovery is thus described:—'We seemed to be on the brink of an awful abyss, from whence were vomited up volumes of hot steam and suffocating vapors. Loud rumbling noises and a peculiar bubbling sound saluted our ears; noxious sulphurous gases filled our nostrils. Altogether, the sight was so strange, so unexpected, and wonderful that many minutes elapsed before we were able to speak to each other.'

The island is well watered with many rivers and streams, all of which teem with excellent fish, the grey mullet (*Mugit viretitus*) being most numerous.

Along the banks of some of the rivers may occasionally be seen disciples of old Izaak Walton plying the gentle art; and the intense satisfaction and great good humor with which they lay on the sward a "half-pounder" mountain mullet, and then glance round with a "Look you,

Master, what I have done!" would warm the heart of Piscator himself.

From meteorological observations recorded in 1877, in the town of Roseau, it was found that the mean temperature for the year was 80° F. The maximum temperature occurred on September 13th when 94° F. was read off, and the minimum temperature 62° F. was recorded on February 7th. It is thus seen that the extreme range was 32°. The mercury, however, rarely reaches 90 F. even during the hottest season, and 94° F. is an exceptionally high temperature. At two thousand feet above the sea, one day in April, 1875, the maximum temperature was 64 F. and the minimum 56 F.

The change of scene worked in a short time by heavy tropical rains is marvellous, and it is a wonderful sight to see the river which was meandering peacefully through the smiling valley transformed in a few hours into a raging torrent, the yellow flood with a loud roar sweeping down to the sea with irresistible fury, carrying along large trunks of trees, and dashing huge boulders down its rocky bed."

Our Shirt Repairing.

Chapter VI.

THE FRENCH ISLANDS.

THREE or four islands that belong to France lie sandwiched in between two of the British West Indies. Indeed, a great portion of the charm that a voyage down here possesses, is due to the fact that within a very short space of time and distance, one may change not only the nationality of the country he is in, but the customs, manners and surroundings as well.

To go from Spain to Denmark, from Denmark to England, from England to France, and back again to British territory, to do all this within three hundred miles of travel, and to find in each outlying island the country to which it belongs far more strongly national and characteristic in its customs than the fatherland itself, is what one can only do in the West Indies.

Emigrants who come here from Europe rarely return. They preserve and transmit to their descendants the ways and manners of the homeland as a part of their patrimony, and since they themselves may never live there more, they build around them as close an imitation as circumstances permit. By years of practice these circumstances become accented, and things that are most strongly marked in the fatherland become more and more developed and pronounced, till the Cuban becomes twice a Spaniard, a Barbadian three times an Englishman, and a Martiniquien four times a Frenchman. Thus we have in each of these islands that we successively visit, an epitome of the country

VIEW OF GUADELOUPE, FROM MASONIC TEMPLE.

to which it belongs presented to us in a concentrated way that is perhaps more completely illustrative of the lands to which they belonged than would be a residence in Europe.

So within six hours after leaving England behind at Dominica, we step ashore in France at Guadeloupe, and in France of the last century.

Nothing is more peculiarly Gallic than the first view of a street in Point-à-Pitre. There are these exceptions it is true ; that most people we meet are black instead of white, that the sun that shines upon us is perpetual instead of intermittent, and that the temperature is many degrees higher than in even the sunny parts of France ; but the tongue we hear is French, the language that is spoken is pure, and barring a certain accent that seems as if it may have been borrowed from the hot land where we listen, one might close his eyes and be at Marseilles.

Beneath the rays of a tropical sun that beat down upon our unaccustomed heads with fury, these Frenchmen wear black clothes and silk hats, and stroll about the streets under the shade of sun umbrellas when the thermometer marks ninety at coolest time of day.

Our tourists paid small attention to such trifles as sun or heat, pervading the streets of this Franco-Indian town with so much celerity and perseverance as to give the idea that their numbers were scores in place of four. They captured carriages of our guides, carrying each in hand a French phrase book from which they manufactured sentences so extraordinary in sound and accent that the amused natives took their money, guessed at what they wanted, handed out a mixture of cool drinks and all parties were content.

That novel experience to Americans of wine served free at dinner in any desired quantity, first made its appearance to us at Point-à-Pitre, and our young gentlemen, winking at each other as they sat down at table at the pleasant "Hotel des Bains," drew each to himself a quart bottle of claret, filled a brimming glass and proceeded to dine as pleased as possible. Before the meal was finished they had taken care of more wine than they had of food, and the result of general extreme hilarity suited so well the temperament of the natives that a profound friendship was struck up and cemented by more flowing bowls and noisy shouting of the "Marseillaise" and "Star Spangled Banner" in frightful combination.

One of the most attractive places to visit in Guadeloupe, guided by a Freemason, is the Masonic Temple at Point-à-Pitre. Upon a hill within the town a building of Egyptian style has been erected, the grounds around which comprise the entire elevation. At the foot a wall separates this land from outside territory, and the whole of the enclosure is devoted to Masonic purposes, where there is a home furnished for the wandering brother who finds himself drifting in this far-off land. Since heretics may not be buried in Catholic countries in consecrated soil, these brothers of the order that knows no religion except that independent of any sect, have laid out within their grounds a pretty cemetery where any one who dies within their jurisdiction, belonging to the fraternity, may be buried in ground that is holier than any blessed by the church.

It is difficult in so short a stay as I made in Guadeloupe to ascertain much about its sanitary condition, or diseases of the island, but as it is unlikely that American tourists will do more than pay a flying visit here, a few words are all that may be necessary.

Within the last few years both Guadeloupe and Martinique have been ravaged by small-pox. Following the example of the mother country, where compulsory vaccination has never been the rule, they have not attempted to enforce it, and the result was a frightful epidemic. This has

RIVER VIEW, MARTINIQUE.

now disappeared, I believe more from lack of material than any other cause, and the islands are in a state of health.

I noticed particularly open sewers continually flushed by rapid streams of mountain water that carry all impurities promptly to the sea, and even in the most crowded parts of the town there are no unpleasant odors whatever.

Such a thing as a closet, as we understand the word, does not exist in these two islands, with the sole exception of one or two in club house or private dwelling, and the primitive method of using tubs which are emptied every morning at daylight into the swift streams by the street-side, is still in vogue.

Food of all kinds is plentiful and cheap, and one may board at the first hotels here or in Martinique, with comfortable rooms and all service, for two dollars a day.

Drives out of town are numerous and attractive, and a party may hire a two-horse carriage for about four dollars a day, which will carry three persons beside the driver. They will find their coachman communicative and intelligent, ready to tell them of the places that they pass, and keep them amused from start to finish; only some one, or all of the party must speak French, for a knowledge of the English language is so great a rarity that I only found in my wanderings about town a single native who could speak our tongue, and that was a servant at the hotel.

The artist will find in all the towns of this island plenty of quaint objects of a past age, plenty of bits of exquisite scenery to occupy his pencil for many a day; and some of the photographs that I brought thence have been admired, not only for their artistic beauty, but for the wealth of suggestion that they contain.

I would advise any one who can find time to spare, to spend a couple of weeks in this curious, quaint, and attractive island. He will find in the American Consul at Point-à-Pitre an intelligent, courteous gentleman, whose long residence there has made him almost a Frenchman, while he has not forgotten his love for his native New England, nor to show warm hospitality to his wandering countrymen.

This gentleman has been removed since my last visit in 1891, and I do not know who his successor is.

From Guadeloupe to Martinique is but a beautiful twelve hours' sail. When the first stars of a tropic night are gleaming from the sky that is so dark a blue as to be almost black, the steamer gets its anchor and heads away to the southward for the island of Josephine. While yet these same stars shine, mingling their light with the morning sun, the ship skirts along under a rocky and bold coast, whose contours of soft roundness are sharply alternated with peaks, rocks, dark gorges, and streams that leap hundreds of feet directly to the sea.

The bay of St. Pierre is one of the most picturesque in these beautiful islands; but it must be understood that this is only one of several that Martinique possesses, and that although the city we now approach is the leading one of commerce, and the largest in population, it is not the capital, nor has it that harbor that has made Martinique an object of envy to every power that owns territory down here. Yet the picture is a beautiful one; and whoever sees the morning sun rise over mountain peaks behind the town for the first time, scattering shadows that have concealed cathedral towers, red-tiled roofs, and tall palms like curving plumes, and touching the shining water with polished lances of light, will not be likely to forget the harbor of St. Pierre.

Like Guadeloupe, the landing is essentially French. Boats of every description surround the ship, and every boatman shouts his loudest in his native tongue, "*Prenez moi, Monsieur, je suis le premier.*"

The most extraordinary apparatus in the shape of boat that mortal eye ever beheld, dances around the anchored ship at St. Pierre. It resembles nothing so much in all this world

BAY OF ST. PIERRE.

as a small coffin made of rough boards, with the top left off. The occupant, however, far from being dead, is the liveliest little darkey that it is possible to conceive. He paddles his funny boat from shore with his hands, and sits upon its bottom as destitute of clothes as when he was born, ready to dive like a frog for the smallest coin that may be thrown him from the deck above. He always gets it, too.

From the landing-place to the Hotel des Bains is but a short walk, scarcely impeded by a visit to the custom-house, whose officers are so polite to tourists that they never open any trunks at all, and mark them "All right," with a courteous wish that our stay in the island may be pleasant.

The first view of a French West Indian hotel is a revelation of oddity to a stranger. Outside it presents no especial difference from other houses in the block. Inside one finds a paved court and an immense cage where fowls of various kinds are waiting their call to serve as parts of the dinner each day. Why this cage exists none can tell, for its doors are always open, and the fowls amuse themselves by excursions into the various sleeping-chambers, to which they have free access day and night.

All the rooms open inward on galleries, and if at any time one needs a servant, he steps out and calls for Marie or Justine, as the case may be. If she is away upon an errand, some one answers for her, "*Tout de suite, Monsieur,*" which means anywhere from half an hour to half a day. If she is there she replies, "*On viens, Monsieur,*" and is forthwith at your door.

The very moderate charge of $2 per diem means bed and three good meals a day — wine and service included — and I am bound to say that all were content. The first breakfast is brought to the room at 6 o'clock, and one eats enough of rolls, Danish butter, soft boiled eggs, and delicious coffee with milk, to last till the regular breakfast comes at noon. This is an elaborate meal of six or seven courses, with plenty of good claret, differing only from dinner — that comes at seven — in the latter having soup to begin with, and a few more courses. After dinner a cigar and chat for the gentlemen, and then comes bed; and by nine o'clock the town is asleep.

It is true that minor annoyances of insects are by no means absent. Cockroaches the size of mice, that travel over the bare floor in the dark; centipedes six inches long, that are now and then killed under one's dining-table, are at first annoying, but one soon learns to make light of them, as they never do any real harm. Spiders are of prodigious dimensions in all these tropical islands. My friend Garesche, the gentlemanly American consul, showed one in his drawing-room that had remained patiently in position upon the ceiling for several weeks. "When he gets hungry," said the Consul, "he comes down, hunts up one or two cockroaches, and is content for an indefinite time thereafter to remain quiet at his post."

After the first breakfast was over, we found amusement plenty in wandering about the quaint, curious streets, looking in the little shops that were filled with things strange to Northern eyes, and inflicting upon the polite owners a series of questions in what we were pleased to call French; or, calling a carriage—and, as in Guadeloupe, one may have a double team here all day for $4 that will carry three beside the driver—start for a journey amongst some of the most attractive scenery that the world knows.

Without being hot at any time, the air is simply delicious in the morning. It comes pure and sweet from the lofty mountains around the town, mingling with the fresh water of the clouds, and the salt sea-breeze from the ocean, at a temperature which, during our entire stay, did not exceed 80° at the highest, and sharply fell from that point as we climbed the mountain roads, until within an hour's drive from the hotel to Morne Rouge, we found light overcoats comfortable, and my pocket thermometer 66° at noonday.

One of these delightful drives carried us to one of the famous medicinal baths of the world. It is called *Les Fontaines Chaudes*, and lies in a deep gorge that cleaves the island's surface from mountain peak to sea, some twelve miles distant from town.

The only difficulty that I found with these thermal springs as a resort, was, that from the last point attainable to the Springs Hotel it was necessary to walk or be carried over a rough road of about a quarter of a mile. The road has been so far improved since this was written that carriages now go quite to the baths. At the springs is comfortable accommodation for a numerous party. The water is strongly sulphurous, at a temperature of 105° where it enters the swimming baths, and 95° where it leaves them. The basins are large and well cared for, separate accommodations being provided for men and women. A medical man has charge of them, and of the hotel as well, and he assured me that some really wonderful cures of rheumatism and allied diseases were effected. He gave me an analysis of the water, which showed its percentage of sulphur in gaseous form to be as large as any on record. It contains besides, silica, lime, and soda to an appreciable extent, and one feels after leaving the bath, where no soap is used, as if he had been oiled from head to foot.

Another delightful excursion is the one to Fort de

A FAIR MARTINIQUIENNE.

France, the ancient capital of the island, and still the residence of the Governor. Here is a magnificent harbor, almost land-locked, with immense capacity inside, and surrounded by lofty peaks that shut off all danger even from hurricanes. In the middle of the great square that is the chief attraction of the place, stands a beautiful marble statue, of the Empress Josephine, erected to her memory by Napoleon III. She was born at the little hamlet of Trois Islets, farther on across the bay, and the place is more alive with memories of this woman than is even our own Mount Vernon with souvenirs of Washington.

Around Fort de France there are also numerous thermal springs. access to which is easy, but they do not possess either swimming baths or a hotel close by.

I found these two islands singularly destitute of lepers in the streets. Making inquiry of one of the leading physicians, I was told that the disease scarcely exists — at least in comparison with the English islands — and that as soon as a case appeared it was promptly isolated; nor was there, during our visit, any epidemic disease whatever.

At the time of year that includes winter months there is no such thing as fever, and moderate precautions as to diet and exposure to heated mid-day sun are sufficient to insure to visiting strangers continued health.

At home, one hears on every hand stories of poisonous serpents of Martinique, that are called the iron lance *(le lance de fer)*. That there are numbers of these snakes in the island is doubtless true, for the records show some twenty-five deaths per annum from their bite among native negroes; yet, in several visits to Martinique, and continual wandering over its beautiful roads, I have never made the personal acquaintance of a single living specimen. During one of my visits I offered a reward for one of them, alive or dead, but none were forthcoming, and the only one I ever saw was a specimen mounted for exhibition at the botanical garden. There is no more danger from serpents in Martinique than there is in the Adirondack region.

Nights are invariably cool and refreshing, and the trade wind blows so strongly through sleeping rooms that a blanket covering was very comfortable during our entire stay.

In place of the light clothing one expects to see, gentlemen of these islands wear conventional black, and appear comfortable therein, while the ladies rarely use for street wear anything thinner than one sees on Broadway or Chestnut Street in May.

In the market and funny little shops around it there are specimens of native crockery made at Trois Islets, which are very odd and pretty. The clay burns into a lemon yellow glaze with streaks of chocolate brown, and fifty cents will buy enough to carry to a host of friends at home.

Since this chapter was written, Martinique has been ravaged by a terrible hurricane, which destroyed the greater part of the town of St. Pierre, all of the village of Morne Rouge, and ruined the island as a tourist resort. Only two years before, Fort de France was half burned up — and there is not at present, January, 1892, a hotel where a visitor may be made comfortable. But this is, of course, a temporary state of things alone, and so profitable a business as caring for tourists will not long be neglected.

MARTINIQUE, April, 1891.

Chapter VII.

BARBADOS.

IN all the West Indies, considered as a winter home for invalids, there is no island so important as the one we are now to visit.

All others have some peculiar attractions and characteristic value; this seems to combine many of the former, and to add to the latter some new features that are entirely its own. Situated as it is out of the line of curvature that marks the chain of mountain peaks extending from Northern to Southern Continental America, which we have grown to regard as the only remaining traces of a lost continent, its geological formation differs radically from them all. It is entirely a land that has been built by the unremitting and prolonged labor of animals, and as is common with such islands, it possesses a drainage peculiarly good, an almost entire absence of hills and valleys, a slight growth of forest, and a surface almost level and slightly elevated from the sea.

It has, from its discovery, been the only one of the islands that has continuously remained in possession of the mother country.

From its first settlement it has been the home of an educated and civilized body of colonists, who have studied its capability in the light of every modern advantage, and have made it what they claim it is, an epitome of England.

In its teeming population (and there is no spot on earth, not excepting China, so thickly settled), nothing in the way of schools or means of advance has been forgotten. From

HARBOR STREET, BRIDGETOWN. — BARBADOS.

its university, which is in close relation with two great English schools, down through its high school and those of lower grade, the utmost possible care has been taken to bring the level of education of its inhabitants to the standard of older countries. People who went there first, carried with them their habits of thrift and comfort, and in the new land where climate was no obstacle to full development, they have succeeded in erecting a class of homes both for themselves and visitors, superior in every way to those of the other islands whose advantages have not been so great.

There is nothing that an Englishman takes greater care of than his personal comfort, and I found in Barbados that this item essential to the traveling invalid had been so thoroughly cared for as to leave little to desire. Even an American hotel is not lacking, kept by an American manager, with poor meals served upon the American plan; a large, handsome, airy building, capable of accommodating three hundred or more guests, with some of the comforts that we are accustomed to find in our hotels at home, and a few of the luxuries. It is true that with the American hotel, American prices have come to the island, and it is out of the question that one can be housed at the Marine, without paying about as much as he would at a first-class New York or Philadelphia hotel. There are, however, several native institutions of the kind where the usual island rates prevail, and where one may live as comfortably as possible for the regulation two dollars a day.

Besides the hotels in the city of Bridgetown, there are others on the northern coast; notably the Crane, where Armstrong made me more completely comfortable than I had ever been before at a Barbadian hotel. The air and temperature are delightful, and one enjoys the luxury of a quiet rest with dry skin as a rarity in the West Indies. I strongly recommend the Crane. There is also a pleasant boarding house at Bathsheba, which would be attractive if it were not perched upon the top of a steep hill, where only good walkers care to climb. Either of these places can be reached by telephone from Bridgetown, and rooms engaged.

There are no surface streams in Barbados, but beneath the white coral that forms the roads and the main part of the island, many feet below the surface, there are rivers of considerable dimensions that circulate in caves, and from one of these, pure fresh water is now supplied in abundance to the city of Bridgetown.

Surface drainage is almost unknown. The porous nature of the land makes any extensive system of sewerage quite unnecessary, and in the most crowded sections of the town one may walk about between the thickly built cabins of the blacks, without meeting anything offensive to sight or smell; and this perfection of natural drainage is one of the greatest advantages to invalids that the island possesses. The next is its freedom from mountains and valleys. Unobstructed, the steady trade winds that have come across the sea for thousands of miles sweep from one side of the island to the other, and carry away with them on their kindly currents every atom of miasm and every sign of poisonous vapors. From morning until night, and all the night long, these winds search out through the slightly built and always open houses every corner and cranny, and cleanse them with a besom that knows no stay. Absence of trees to any considerable amount, adds to the general healthfulness of the land by avoiding obstruction to unremitting play of the beneficent trades.

For this same reason the temperature of Barbados is a particularly steady one. During several weeks of residence upon the island my thermometer marked an average through the day of seventy-eight, with a fall of ten degrees each night. Through the hottest hours, and these were from eleven to four, there would be a rise of ten degrees, and the sun, almost vertical, was reflected back from the white streets and house walls with a force that needed to be protected against; but the winds were so strong, so steady, and carried away from the surface of the body the insensible and sensible perspiration so fast, that the sensation produced was one of comparative mildness, and danger of sun-stroke to the unaccustomed visitor was greater than it would have been with a higher temperature, without the steady breeze.

One of my party, who was unacquainted with this peculiarity of Barbados, started for a walk in the middle of one of those bright days, from the Marine hotel to the centre of the town, a distance of about a mile, without the protection of a sun umbrella, which no native would have neglected; he paid for his carelessness by a sharp attack of sun-stroke, and although almost a year has passed, the effects of that blow have not been recovered from. Every one who goes into the street at mid-day, should carry a protection over his head against these powerful, vertical rays. It is better, however, to avoid walking, where cab fare is as cheap as there, and where animals are accustomed to the heat.

The approach to the island is one of extreme beauty. When the traveler has for a week past been studying pictures of scenery of mountain and glen; has been watching in living volcanoes and riven rocks evidences of terrible

ARROWROOT MILL, BARBADOS.

forces that have buried a continent, and has been growing accustomed to types of flowers and animals peculiar to volcanic lands, the change is as great as it is pleasant. To the formation of all other islands of the group, to the especial beauties that one has to climb thousands of feet to find, to the deep forests and hill lakes of Dominica, Saint Lucia and Martinique, Barbados is an exception dressed in light green and white.

Approaching its soft slopes from the westward, one is strongly reminded of carefully cultivated English hills, an illusion which disappears only when the harbor is entered, and while running down the coast from the North, there are few things to mark the difference — at least from twenty miles away.

No mountain ranges accentuate outlines that grow blue as they recede until lost in the bluer sky; no patches of dark color mark where thick forests lie, and no signal gleam from falling water shows where a white cascade catches sun rays and sends them back to the watcher to tell where it lies hidden in mountain gorge.

Every acre of land is light green or snow-white at that distance, with dividing lines of color marking fields; and with a strong glass these outlines are resolved into trim farms, with windmills or tall chimneys for steam boilers to give the needed working power. Drawing closer, the land becomes characteristic, and it is plain that a new formation is before us.

There is nothing ancient in these low hills of coral stone, or shelving shores; nothing that appeals to the geologist or naturalist; only a new world for the student of human nature, who finds in this library — whose volumes are mostly bound in black, many a pleasant problem to be worked out beneath a lovely sky and with genial surroundings.

As we sailed into Carlisle bay, the harbor of the island, early in last February, an air of prosperity and business was seen at once. More than a hundred sail of many flags were anchored, among them a noble British squadron of nine men-of-war. Boats were pulling about in every direction, and speedily surrounded us to tout for passengers ashore, as we carefully sidled to our position and let go anchor. They carried any and everything, those boats, invariably demanding double fare at first — the custom hereabouts. But we were used to that, and a shilling apiece was all they got. Before us lay the city of Bridgetown, low in buildings, red as to roofs, spread out three miles in length by two inland, dominated by a cathedral tower and half hidden in greenery. Rounding the breakwater, called the careenage — for they tip vessels half over, here, to scrape them clean — we ran alongside a stone quay and were ashore, to be surrounded by a crowd of darkies intent upon earning a penny from the new-comers. "Here am I, master!" "Your boy John, master!" "I's Uncle Sam boy William, master!" "Dis de way to de ice-house master!" *Et usque ad nauseam.*

Most travelers who come here report the negroes insolent, devoid of education, and bristling with petty annoyance. It is odd, perhaps, but I have never seen all this. They are persistent, it is true; but where human life is crowded as here, and pennies are hard to get, why should they not be? During a stay of weeks in Barbados, I have always found the blacks polite and accommodating, even to each other.

No fault can be found with the food supply in quantity or quality. Besides most of those vegetables which we are familiar with at home, there are one or two others that grow only here, of which the natives are very fond. One is the eddo, which resembles closely our oyster plant.

I think that the density of population is what impresses a stranger most. It is like living aboard a man-of-war, where men are as thick as bees, and space for another one seems difficult to find. There is absolutely no privacy. Out from the town of Bridgetown, as far as you choose to go, there are little boxes of houses along the wayside, each holding a numerous family, while troops of negroes stroll along the white way. Sit for a moment beneath a lignum-vitæ or bread-fruit shade, and negroes spring up from the ground to gaze and wonder who you are. This teeming, concentrated human life is the first novelty that a visitor sees.

In an area of one hundred and sixty-six square miles, one hundred and eighty thousand human beings live — and, apparently live comfortably well. It is, perhaps, the most densely-peopled territory known, and this state of affairs makes itself evident at once in every part of the island.

Streets are crowded from building to building all day long, as a New York pavement is in the forenoon. The people are almost all good-humored blacks, clean, and neatly dressed in white. My driver, William, went through this mass at a steady trot, and they got out of the way easily, without a word of such abuse as is common in northern towns, not often needing his warning, "Look out da! Hi!"

My camera was a continual source of wonderment. They know that "De master takes pictures wid dat masheen," but that is all, and its production in the most secluded spot imaginable would bring together within two minutes an audience large, attentive, admiring, but never annoying.

They live very simply, these children of the sun. For food, fruit, flying fish and yams are nearly enough, are nutritious, and cost but a trifle — say a penny or two a day. For clothes, plain white material, which covers them completely, except feet that are always bare, and an aged straw hat picked up somewhere, is really more than they need in a climate where clothes are a burden, and Edenian attire something to be longed for. Their dress costs little more than fig-leaves.

One of their little houses, in many instances not more than ten feet square, can be rented for about $2 a month, and water is free. So they get on very comfortably, and, except from habit, do not often beg. That your dog should come up and ask for food does not seem more natural than that these negroes should hold out their hand for a penny; and the brute animal takes a refusal with much poorer grace than the human. A stranger driving past (and every visitor bears his cachet upon his forehead) represents wealth, intelligence, and undisputed superior authority. Why should he not be asked for a penny? Clearly, there is no reason whatever.

Probably the best way of living, for a family that comes to stay several months, is to rent a house at Hastings or Fontabelle, the two chief suburbs of Bridgetown, and have their own home. A comfortable house for four or five persons can be found for $25 or $30 a month, and servants, better than ours on the average, can be hired at from $1 to $4 a month. There is no difficulty in getting a pleasant place a mile or two from the town, as horse-cars run to all the principal suburbs; and, once at home in the new climate, its highest advantages may be attained.

Artists will find constant amusement and difficult studies

A PLANTER'S HOME, BARBADOS.

in the peculiar color effects that are so hard to catch. Just wherein it lies I cannot tell; but there is something extraordinary in the light of Barbados. My camera, quite trustworthy at home and in the Western Caribbean, played me strange tricks of over and under exposure upon the same plate. No views out of doors can be made instantaneously, and there is no certainty what the developer will reveal.

And the same disturbing element exists with colors. Black and white quite fail to express tropical effects; and so does the brush — at least, as far as I have seen. One may try as hard as possible to catch the green of yonder breadfruit tree or mass of changing crotons; but before the sketch is done it is usually destroyed, an utter failure. With longer time some one will learn, doubtless; but no one seems to have done it so far.

Driving is a constant delight. Roads of rare excellence wind in and out of shady groves in town, and extend over the island in every direction. Horses are fair and can be hired at reasonable prices; so few people walk. A handsome two-horse landau, carrying five besides the driver, can be secured for $10 a day for a journey of twenty miles each way, which will carry one pretty well across the island.

Cabs are many, and though wretched in appearance, as a rule get one about cheaply enough. Twelve cents a mile is certainly a moderate price for two occupants, and that is what the charge is.

One can have a delicious sea bath at Hastings every day in the year. A reef of coral sand effectually protects swimmers from the immense sharks that infest all these seas, and the water is of a velvety softness that tempts to long indulgence. Daily baths are a necessity where the skin is so active, and a native would sooner neglect his breakfast than his dip.

The leading industry is sugar, and this year's crop is expected to be a phenomenal one, seventy-five thousand tons being the anticipated yield, which, at three cents a pound, will amount to a handsome sum. All the fields of brilliant green are cane, shading up from a delicate pea tint with under color of buff, to a dark grass green, with whose deep shadows the peculiar light of this island plays strange pranks. Sometimes, watching a field, it is almost black, and then, as sunbeams catch it bending over, it will seem red. Through its tall stalks and hanging leaves the ever present breeze sings of bountiful harvest and far away seed time, and then speeds on its way. In these fields there is no silence. One may almost see and hear the growth, so plain is the creaking and rustling that is going on around, so rapid the increase in size.

I was writing one morning about six o'clock at Fontabelle, and although the sun was not quite up, the pervading light that is never entirely absent from Barbados was reflected back from the sea to my table through bread-fruit and palm trees, as soft as from a sunset cloud. My thermometer marked seventy, and nocturnal fragrance was not yet all vanished. Perfumes of roses contended with dying odors of the *la bonita del noche;* and day sounds of birds were taking the place of the night-frog, whose musical double note had scarcely ceased to vibrate. Peace and beauty reigned; and as one deep breath after another of pure, warm air sent blood to finger tips, life, under almost any pressure, seemed well worth living, and lovely earth very hard to part from. The passionate attachment that the simple blacks feel for their native land is easily explained at charming break of day; and a feeling of contentment pervades every nerve of the visitor who has escaped the chilling frosts and deadly winds of northern lands.

Among the best trips, indeed the very best in Barbados, are those by carriage to St. John's Church and Codrington College, and by train to Bathsheba, which lies among the wildest scenery of this coast, whose grandest views cannot be very imposing since the land does not reach the altitude of a thousand feet at any point.

In company with Mr. Grundy, the courteous manager of the Barbados Railway, I once made a visit to the North coast under the most favorable auspices. The little railroad is, itself, a curiosity. Only twenty-one miles long, it has twelve stations that rejoice in most ridiculously inappropriate names; and at every one of them the same relative amount of form and ceremony was gone through as if a train was leaving Liverpool for London. A black grenadier wore a helmet marked "Railway Police," and scared away small loafing darkeys with majestic wave of hand or suggestive touch of rattan. Porters, with their duty printed in big, red letters on cap-ribbons, rushed about among the six passengers that were going with us, as busily as if a thousand trunks were awaiting demolition; and shouted out, "This train leaves for Rouen, Windsor, etc., etc.," with as much pomp as if it were actually starting for those very places in Europe. In a third-class carriage in front, a lot of jolly tars from H. M. S. *Pylades* were off for a day in the country where sugar cane grows and rum is plentiful. One of them had a guitar, and we presently heard a song, whose chorus ended with "From Scilly to Ushant is forty-five leagues."

Barbados is everywhere healthful, but when one feels depressed or exhausted with Bridgetown heat, or needs a little rest from hospitable attention, the Crane hotel with its cliffs and its delightfully cool nights, offers a change that few other West Indian places are able to present.

Among the many insects that fly about evening lamps and in pleasant gardens outside, I noticed a painful lack of brilliant colors. No painted moths nor shining fire-flies are to be seen, and the latter are unknown; so that the island offers none of the attractions to an entomologist that are so many in Venezuela.

Poisonous reptiles are few and scarce; and St. Patrick must have made a flying trip to Barbados, as far as snakes are concerned. I heard of a few centipedes and scorpions, but they are found only in the neighborhood of sugar estates, scarcely ever being seen in town, so that people who fear inter-tropical lands in general, as homes for venomous serpents and insects, may put their apprehensions aside if they conclude to go to this island.

One thing we had come to see was what is called the animal flower cave, a collection of actiniæ in one of the caverns that dashing water has worn in the rock face, far below surface level, by years of steady toil.

No place, this, for women; so our ladies returned to the carriage and marooned it awhile, which is Barbadian for recuperation physical, while we climbed down a stony sort of chasm, until before us, a little way across, was the cave opening, and leading to it a narrow path along a ridge, steep, and wet, with hungry looking waves rushing over it at irregular intervals. The guide watched his chance, darted over with a whoop; and watching ours, we followed. The tail end of a ferocious swell caught one fellow and I thought he was gone, but he escaped with a sound wetting, and we called him clumsy.

Inside, the floor was tolerably dry and quite safe, so after a little more abuse for our friend who had scared us so, we went into an inner chamber, and there in a circular basin

IN A TROPICAL GARDEN.

with a stone floor, reposed a still pool of liquid glass. Now and then its shining surface was gently stirred by trickling streams falling into it, but it was almost incredible that water should be so transparent as this. Where there was no motion, nothing visible parted eye from crevices in that floor, six feet below.

We gathered around, looking quietly at the water, when what had appeared to be the dead stem of a water-lily near me began to expand. "Look!" I whispered, in fear of spoiling the show; and in twenty seconds that pool seemed a blazing garden of flowers. With a prevailing color of yellow, of the tint of buttercups, there was enough of red and blue to make purple hues also, which changed as we gazed enchanted, with each slight motion of the plants.

Finally, Jack plunged his hand in after the nearest one, and, presto! the garden was gone, the pool was empty again.

Quiet for a moment, and the play began once more, and so we had various acts, all alike. We were in hopes that the colors might change, but they were ever the same.

To make this excursion, some preparation is needed. The tide must be right, guides engaged, and the sea must have been quiet for some time. I was four weeks waiting for the trip before all things were ready.

It is a bad place for rheumatism. Night and day the skin is working to its utmost capacity, and an unnoticed chill stiffens up muscles that refuse with painful persistence to be loosened. For those who seek dissipation, who ask "What is there to do down there?" and who demand ceaseless occupation, Barbados is no place.

There is no theatre, no amusement of any kind, and the only departure from such mild fun as driving and sailing furnish, is taken at a social, well-served dinner or a pleasant dance, where each knows all the other guests.

But for quiet, rest and healthfulness, there is but one island of the Atlantic comparable with this, and there, Americans find little except climate, and that rated at four dollars a day.

The suggestions that I have previously made for clothing to be worn on other islands, are equally forcible here, with the exception that one can purchase garments made in excellent style and of the very best English goods, for what seems to be a ridiculously small price. For several years past I have had all my summer suits made here, paying for a first-class article from thirteen to fifteen dollars complete, and for an evening dress suit twenty-five dollars. Lady friends who were with me, fairly revelled in the cheapness of goods. A first-class dress-maker would come and measure her customer at the hotel, bring back the costume complete without ever trying it on, and charge four dollars for an ordinary suit, for one made of silk or finer goods with any amount of trimming, six dollars. Of course these prices would not include linings or thread, both of which were purchased by the customer as cheaply as other goods. In these days of increasing prices from tariff vagaries, it is refreshing in the highest degree to be able to purchase a suit of ladies' gear complete for seven or eight dollars, and if upon arriving home changes are necessary to fit them to the reigning fashion, it is likely that the least of these will cost more than the original price of the costume.

The only thing that cannot be bought here for American women is shoes, for English feet, both male and female, are larger than American, and care must be taken to carry a sufficient supply of foot-gear to last.

There is nothing more beautiful in the world than tropical

play of color over the western sea beneath a setting sun. At Barbados the only difficulty that artists find in interpreting it is to obtain from their color boxes tints sufficiently brilliant, and if they do succeed in even a moderate degree in representing the glory of these sunsets, they are sure to be charged with manufacturing in the most absurd manner, combinations that cannot be even dreamed of by those not fortunate enough to have seen them.

This island is a health resort in summer as well as in winter. Invalids from South America and from the neighboring islands, resort here for coolness in July and August, as we of the frozen North for genial warmth in winter months. The result is a constant study on the part of the inhabitants of the wants and needs of travelers, with an effect that is especially comforting to those who go there.

Medical men are thoroughly qualified, competent, and courteous gentlemen, and receive their colleagues from America with a hospitality that is refreshing to a stranger.

I noticed a few lepers in the streets of Bridgetown, and learned from my friend Dr. Archer, that owing to the careful and stringent sanitary regulations in force, with isolation of these unfortunates, that they have been almost banished from the island and driven from the public streets.

Travelers going to Barbados this winter will fare better than we did last, for extra steamers have been placed upon the lines, with better accommodations and greater comforts. The only warning that I can give to those who think of going there is, that no one of the islands, not even this one, is a fit place for rheumatism in any form, or for advanced lung disease.

FONTABELLE, BARBADOS, April, 1891.

Chapter VIII.

TRINIDAD.

FIRST in size, last in the chain of islands that unites North and South America, largest and most varied in beauty of all the Leeward and Windward groups, Trinidad next calls for our attention.

It is lovely in the distance, whether approached from seaward across the broad Atlantic, or from the other islands through which our readers have been following us for so long a time. The three lofty peaks that gave the island its name, "The Trinity," still rise from masses of deep green to tell why; and still the traveler, from whatever land, exclaims in his tongue, as did Columbus in musical Castilian, "*Que isla gloriosa!*"

With the exception of Jamaica, there is more variety of climate accessible to tourists and invalids in this island than in any other; for it has thriving and pleasant towns in many parts, at different elevations. In so large an area as this, some 1,800 square miles of irregular quadrangle, intersected with streams, seamed by mountain chains and traversed by rail, there is necessarily much to see; much to do for busily inclined folks, and quiet rest for those whose strength is not equal to exertion.

Caribs called the island "Iere" in their musical tongue, from glittering humming birds that then, as now, gemmed the dark green of perpetual foliage—and have a pretty story about the Pitch Lake of La Brea and the birds.

There is a diversified geological formation, including that of the palæozoic, tertiary and pliocene ages, with no recent coral formation, except a little around the shores, and a wonderful variety of soil and vegetation. Nowhere are tree ferns — those splendid specimens fifty feet high — found in greater beauty than in Maraccas Valley, and groves of cacao trees in cool shade of bois immortelle, are beautiful beyond compare. Orchids abound; and I was told by collectors that there are some sixty varieties in the island, some of them very rare. An avenue of samang trees that leads from the main road to St. James' barracks, beyond the savanna of Port-of-Spain, is said to be unique in the Western Continent; the trees having been brought as shoots many years ago from Farther India.

In the capital city, there are several excellent hotels. The Family Hotel, the Hotel de Paris, and four or five others, offer all possible comfort at the regular rate of two dollars a day, or ten dollars a week, and one could not be better housed. At the "Paris" good Madame Louise takes personal charge of her guests, and sees that they lack nothing. One gets all native dishes there, and has a chance to try them; while at the "Family," where tourists mostly go, the cuisine is much more English.

Passengers are warned to look out for swindling boatmen. Shallow water compels ships to anchor a long way out, and everything is carried ashore in boats. The only way is to demand the government tariff, or to make a bargain before starting, and the harbor police will see to it that both parties keep to their agreement. Boats will hold three or four passengers, and the regular fare is two shillings

ALMOND WALK, PORT-OF-SPAIN, TRINIDAD.

(50 cents) each; but a party can get ashore for a shilling apiece, including baggage.

The same warning applies to cabmen. I have been asked ten shillings for a drive to Maraval, four miles out, and have gone for three. There is a tariff, but it is too high, and a bargain is much better.

It is hot. Even in St. Joseph or Arima, which I regard as the coolest places in Trinidad, the mercury averages 80° in January and February, rarely falling below 75° at night or ascending above 88° in mid-day. Visitors will find, however, the early morning delicious in freshness, that seems much cooler than the glass indicates, and will draw their wraps around them as the cool trade wind comes in, sifting through thick leaves dripping with dew. Only exertion and improper food make heat oppressive. One who drives regularly, keeps in from mid-day sun, eschews much meat and swears off from all stimulants, will become accustomed to the high thermometer in a day or two, and be happy.

There is excellent society. Owing to the varied population, most Trinidadians are tri-lingual, speaking English, French and Spanish, with equal facility. It is funny enough to hear a little tot half-a-dozen years old, commence a sentence in French, continue in English and wind up in good Castilian, as I have heard more than once in Port-of-Spain. For the same reason, one finds circles of English, Spanish and French society of the first class, entrance into any or all of which is promptly given to the traveler who is properly accredited. Hospitality is unbounded. There is something in the free, open air and genial warmth, that opens people's hearts, and dinners, receptions and the like, are frequent on every hand.

The harbor entrance is dramatic. On either side are lofty

hills that narrow the strait we sail through to a hundred yards, beyond which another sea stretches its serene welcome towards us, from encircling shores so far distant to the south as to be lost in Venezuelan sky. Not one, but many of these

AVENUE OF SAMANG TREES.

openings cleave the ring of land that holds confined this inner lagoon; this great lake that is called the Gulf of Paria. The Spaniards called them Bocas, or mouths, adding such names as circumstances suggested, Monos, from the apes that peopled these hills; or Navios, where ships could go; or Grande, largest of them all; and the names have never been changed. Through these passages a swift tide plays wild pranks upon ships that dare its power driven by sails only, and the bones of one gallant East Indiaman, from among the others that have vanished, still mark the dangers of the Boca de Navios.

To the left, a range of peaks high enough to be visible at a great distance, stretches along the northern coast, and on their southern face deep valleys show like black lines on the green. Swell follows swell, mountain succeeds mountain in blue perspective as we sail nearer, until, entering the ring, we advance upon Trinidad and see the outlines assume different forms, until at last we drop anchor before Port-of-Spain, and prepare to enjoy a visit to Iere, the land of humming birds.

It is a crown colony; that is to say, under direct supervision of the Colonial Secretary at London, without general suffrage. Its late governor, Sir William Robinson, K. C. M. G., is a man of great sagacity, long experience in colonial affairs, and withal a hospitable gentleman of much literary ability; and his charming wife, who is a native of Nassau, presided gracefully over a household into which it was a pleasure to be invited to enter. The governor's attentions to a tourist, an invitation to dinner or a ball, settles one's status everywhere, and he is sure to be heartily welcomed.

Letters of introduction should come from persons well acquainted to prominent men in the island, for of late, speculations in asphalt and cacao have drawn so many down there that residents are compelled to draw the line somewhere, and mere perfunctory credentials are not sufficient.

VILLA LEE, TRINIDAD.

In every direction from the capital are excursions, the greater part of which may be taken with small expenditure of time and money. The one to Maraval I have already mentioned as worth going over a dozen times. A little farther away lies Blue Basin, at the head of Diego Martin Valley, some nine miles from town. It is reached by good roads, which extend almost to the pool, and a carriage should take a party of four out and back for a pound — five dollars. The way leads through the Hindu suburb of La Perou, where is the only Brahmin temple out of Hindostan and its stately baba-jee, chief priest, past the samang avenue of St. James' barracks, out into the country among the cane. The road might be in the suburbs of Bombay or Madras. There is the same straight, white road, bordered by scanty palms, behind which jungle grows close; the same rows of Eastern huts, with brass pans and kettles outside; the same quiet, bright-eyed, clear-featured and straight-haired coolies, with submissive "Salaam, sahib," and the same naked, brown babies, with white lines of caste drawn on forehead or cheek. Leaving the Hindus, the way goes on past little villages, each with its story of murder or violence, told with earnest gravity by negro driver to carefully listening passenger. At last it winds upward beside a dancing brook that is the outlet for Blue Basin, until the carriage is left and there is a hundred feet or so to the brink of the pool. Through lacing vines and clinging ferns some sixty feet above, is seen a patch of blue sky, from the center of which a frightened little brook slides down through shadow in foaming lace to the basin, from which reflected sunlight shines back from a cobalt blue that gives the Basin its name.

Besides the pool for attraction, there are strange plants and flowers, and over all a misty sense of fresh coolness that envelops the valley and makes it a pleasant place to rest after the drive. Heat is excluded by thick greenery, and if visitors have been wise enough to bring luncheon with them from their hotel, nothing prevents a delightful picnic in the hottest part of the day outside.

Shops of Port-of Spain are large and stocks heavy. One can purchase any needed article cheaply, and although prices are not quite as low as at Barbados, they are small enough. I found in one of the tailor's shops a New York cutter who had emigrated and opened a neat shop on the corner, where he made up Broadway garments at Chatham street prices, and made money, too. All sorts of goods, in fact, a sort of Macy's, may be found at the Caledonian House on King street, where everything that is sold in the West Indies is displayed. There are especially fine lawns shown here, made only for the tropics, which our ladies said were simply exquisite and not to be found even in New York.

Here and at Wilson's, just above, may be found specimens of table scarfs and small shawls of Indian make and gorgeous colors, at moderate prices; but there are no curiosities in Trinidad, except the coolie jewelry.

Other things to see in daily drives around town are the fine Government Buildings, with good library, the ornate Police Barracks, the Anglican and Roman Catholic Cathedrals, neither of any beauty inside or out, and the Union Club; especially the Club. My heart goes out in thanks to the kind officers of this hospitable institution, who never fail to extend to a friend or acquaintance the hospitalities of their comfortable home, where they keep up a good restaurant, and retain several chambers at the service of such guests as prefer them to hotels.

Then, besides the great savanna already spoken of, there are numerous lesser open places and park-like streets that give plenty of breathing space for all, including the inevitable turkey-buzzard, whose foul face and curious antics appeal at once to the twin senses of curiosity and disgust, at every turn, on every corner. Nasty as they are, I have had more than one hearty laugh at their clumsy battles and wise looks from watery, blear eyes, as they slowly and reluctantly make way for a passer-by.

To St. Joseph, the ancient capital of Trinidad, one goes by rail now, and when one climbs the hill past Calvary to the pretty plaza he finds himself before as fair a vision of tropical scenery as ever enchanted traveler's eyes. At the foot of a gently sloping hill, a mile away, a double row of water alders, or some such aquatic bush, marks the course of a little stream scarcely more than a brook in size. Yet up this Caroni river Sir Walter Raleigh drove his armed boats from the Gulf of Paria and captured from the Spaniards their chief town; they not believing it possible for any craft, however small, to ascend the stream. In the seventeenth century there was no stopping at trifles among the rovers of the Spanish Main.

Beyond the river, St. Augustine chimneys are the only white that breaks the green clear away to Montserrat Hills, where flaming leaves of bois immortelle change the hues to crimson, and with its miles of spread shows the admiring stranger probably for the first time crimson clouds that grow on trees.

Up here the air is purer than in Port-of-Spain, and I found a blanket comfortable in the early morning, even if the thermometer remained nearly at the same level; and the city is very healthy, as is the whole island, if one is careful. It will hardly do to be exposed to night air with its high dew point, or to indulge in prolonged dissipation, and then call the climate dangerous. Brown, of Cleveland, tried hunting alligators in the swamps by early moonlight, and nearly lost his life thereby with dengue fever. Perhaps he thinks the climate is bad. But there have been no epidemics in Trinidad for years, and with such rigid and well-enforced laws as they have, there is small danger of one.

Whoever goes to St. Joseph must either have a resident acquaintance who can " put him up," or plan to return the same day; for there are no hotels. But as it is only six miles from Port-of-Spain, with many trains, it is easy to go and return before dinner, for there is not much to see. In the Cathedral are some fair statues, and in the churchyard adjoining, an old burial vault dating 1682. When one has seen these, the view from the plaza, and made the Stations of the Cross on Calvary near by, he will be ready to return; unless he have friends there, who will keep him as long as possible.

In the latter case, or in any case indeed, a visit to the famous and great St. Augustine sugar estates will richly repay a visitor, who will see for the first time coolie laborers at work, and watch the manufacture of pure sugar. Every attention is shown to strangers, and their presence heartily welcomed.

If one is fond of riding, nothing can be more charming than an excursion up Maraccas Valley to the Falls, which resemble the Staubbach, only infinitely more beautiful. The round distance is some sixteen miles from St. Joseph, and horses must be arranged for a day or two in advance. Your Port-of-Spain landlord will attend to this, but a material portion of the expense may be saved by addressing J. G.

De Silva, St. Joseph, who is accustomed to arrange these excursions.

Besides the lovely cascade at the end of the journey and its closed gateway of lofty cliffs clad in greens of unknown names, there are beautiful bits all the way, with occasional groups of the tree ferns that are so rare, and no less than seven fords across the dancing stream before we reach the estate La Florida, end of traveled road. Thence, perhaps for an eighth of a mile, people foot it, and it pays.

But of all the trips of the island, the one to the Pitch Lake of La Brea, is the most curious. If you chance to be in Port-of-Spain on Monday or Saturday, you may take advantage of a stumpy little steamer that runs the round trip in one day, and do it quickly; if not, you may go to San Fernando by rail any afternoon, stay over night, and go early in the morning to the lake. There are two hotels, one kept by a funny black woman, who tells her guests that the other one is in charge of "a mizzable nigga', sah. I keeps hotel for de superiorities, sah, and dat ar man for the inferiorities." So I presume that Mrs. Glasson's is the better, and poor enough at that.

It is no part of my plan here to attempt a detailed description of the lake, except to say that any other name than lake would have done as well for such an arid, hot, black, uninteresting plain as we reach after so much trouble, and to add that as reflected heat is excessive from the shining, odorous pitch surface, care must be taken not to stop there too long.

The Mud Volcanoes, as they have named certain mounds of earth some three feet high that are situated near a place called Monkeytown, interested me as promising effective cure for some of the many forms of rheumatism that are common in the tropics, to say nothing of leprosy. But after

ROAD TO PITCH LAKE, TRINIDAD.

a tedious journey to Princes Town and then by horse to the spot, there was nothing but hot water ejected, occasionally muddy, and bursting out with considerable force. A journey there will not pay.

The leper question is admirably cared for in Trinidad. These unfortunates are sequestered in a spacious asylum at Cocorite, a few miles out from Port-of-Spain, under the careful and kind supervision of Dr. Koch who welcomes all American medical men who care to visit his charge. Very few lepers are seen in Trinidad streets, and these are under supervision.

The following interesting account of the Carib Indians, that wonderful race of aborigines that is not yet extinct, in spite of wars with powerful nations and contact with the destructive vices of civilization, was taken from a pamphlet called *A Historical and Descriptive Sketch of the Colony of St. Vincent*, which I have lately received from Capt. Maling, Administrator of the colony.

As a vivid and truthful picture of what is almost a bygone race, it is well worthy a place in this or any other work upon the West Indies:

THE CARIBS.

"When the West Indies were discovered by Columbus the lesser Antilles, that beautiful chain of islands stretching from the 'Virgin' group in lat. 18° 30″ N. to Tobago in lat. 11° 16″ N. in the form of a bow or crescent, were inhabited by Caribs, a branch of the great American Indian race. St. Vincent was found to be very populous 'on account of its being the rendezvous of their expeditions to the continent,' and Dominica situated 2° 20″ further North was apparently the next in importance.

CARIB TYPES, ORINOCO RIVER.

The Caribs were described in the *History of the Caribby Islands*, a valuable book published in 1666, now in the library of the Jamaica Institute, as handsome, well-shaped people, of smiling countenance, middle stature, having broad shoulders and 'most of them in good plight and stronger than the French; their mouths are not over large and their teeth are perfectly white and close; true is, their complexion is naturally of an orange color, and that color spreads even into the whites of their eyes which are black somewhat like those of the Chinese and Tartars, but very piercing.' They had long, black hair, but no beards, which, indeed, seemed never to grow, or if they did were pulled out. Both men and women went perfectly nude and considered clothing ridiculous. Sometimes, as a matter of courtesy, they were said to put on clothing when going amongst the Europeans but took it off again as soon as they returned. They bathed every day and dyed their bodies with Annotto (Roucou) which was said to harden the skin, keep it very smooth and protect the body from heat and cold and from the bites of mosquitoes, and drew dark lines about the face and eyes, but on particular occasions they used other colors as well over face and body. The men decorated their heads with crowns of different feathers; sometimes wore scarves of feathers, etc., thrown over the shoulders, or girdles of the same, hanging down to the middle of the thighs; round the necks, were, in some cases, whistles made out of the bones of their enemies, or chains made of the teeth of the Agouti, and the chiefs wore medals of polished copper called *Caracolis*, bracelets round the upper part of the arm near the shoulders, and chains of *Rassada* round the legs. The women pierced the upper lip and inserted bodkins of bone, and wore rings or bits of crystal through the cartilage separating the nostrils, necklets, bracelets of amber or coral on the wrists, and buskins of rushes and cotton reaching to the ankles.

The custom of flattening the foreheads of the infants obtained amongst the Caribs as amongst the other tribes of the American Indian race, and the skulls found in St. Vincent show this distinguishing mark.

They were intrepid mariners and of very warlike tastes; courtly in manners, and never refusing to strangers the cassava or native bread and water in time of peace, when the demon of war was aroused they became fiends, treacherous, cruel, vindictive, massacring their enemies when captured and consuming their flesh as food. Columbus is alleged, while exploring the shores of Guadeloupe in November, 1493, to have discovered numerous traces of cannibalism, and amongst others, ' human limbs suspended to the beams of the houses as if curing for provisions; the head of a young man recently killed, was yet bleeding; some parts of his body were roasting before the fire, others boiling with the flesh of geese and parrots.'

The religious beliefs of the Caribs were very simple and primitive. Sorcerers were held in great esteem by them, and the rude carvings of the sun and moon found on the rocks in St. Vincent and Grenada, seem to indicate that they were made for purposes of worship. Their traditions as to the origin of their tribes as related to M. Du Montel were twofold. One story represented them as inhabitants of Florida under the name of Cofachites whose only belief was in the evil spirit ' *Mabouya*,' but having made a successful invasion of the territory of the Apalchites, who were sun worshippers, and taken up their residence there, the tribe became divided on the question of adopting sun worship and a section were expelled, who after much wandering reached the sea, and hearing from some islanders who were driven ashore by stress of weather that there were other uninhabited islands to the south of theirs, they sailed in search of them to discover a home for themselves and landed at the island of Santa Cruz, which they named 'Ayay,' from whence they spread southwards. This story represents the word 'Caraibes' to mean 'Stranger' in the language of the Apalchites. The other tradition was that all the Caribs were subject to the Arovagues of Trinidad and the mainland in the vicinity, but rebelled and went to live on the islands, and that in their language Caribbean meant 'rebel.'

Between these islands they traversed the ocean in their canoes and pirogues for fishing purposes or for war, gathering at their rendezvous at St. Vincent, and from thence proceeding along the islands of the Grenadines, Grenada and Tobago (which latter place does not seem to have been regularly inhabited, but appears to have been used as a place of call for provisions and water, or a base of operations) to make incursions against the Arovagues of the continent. The Caribs who had not advanced further than the civilization of the age of stone, and used the bow and arrows as their weapon of war and the chase, poisoned their arrows with the juice or milk found between the bark and the wood of the manchineel tree, the juice of its fruit, the dew falling from its leaves mixed with other ingredients.

The Caribs had not, during the period of over three centuries of contact with Europeans, progressed very materially in civilization. They had doubtless adopted certain of their customs such as the wearing of clothing, etc., but it was not until 1792 that Sir William Young, in the journal of his visit to St. Vincent, and speaking of the chief Duvallé, before alluded to, said: 'he is the most enlightened of the Caribs and may be termed the founder of civilization among them.' The events that followed only four years after may lead one to conclude without injustice that this civilization was but skin deep.

The remnants of this interesting race are still to be found in St. Vincent, the number returned in the last census being 192. The true Caribs, who, in contradistinction to the Black Caribs, are locally called the Yellow Caribs, renting land at a place called Sandy Bay, on the windward coast under the nominal control of a headman named Henry Morgan. They have abandoned their former habits, and with the exception of perhaps two or three forgotten their language. They earn their living as boatmen or fishermen, in cultivating small patches of garden ground for themselves, and as basket-makers, an art in which they excel, and which they are said to have preserved from the teaching of their ancestors. These baskets which are made in nests, fitting into one another, are so constructed as to be water-tight and to last for years. The people are perfectly fearless on the water and are the principal boatmen employed in shipping sugar on the dangerous windward coast. The little boys lash two bits of log together, erect a small pole between them, and put out to sea to catch fish, sitting astride of this floating apparatus. Anything that comes to their hands is tied to the pole for safety. Sometimes this aquatic rocking horse is toppled over by a wave and the rider gets an involuntary bath; but he soon rights his steed again and is astride of him as if nothing had happened.

The Black Caribs reside on the leeward side of the island at Morne Ronde under a grant of occupancy. They elect a headman from time to time, the present one being John François. All matters of dispute are referred to the rector of the Parish, from whose decision appeal lies to the Governor, and it is very seldom that they have recourse to the ordinary Law Courts. There is also another settlement of Black Caribs at a place called Greigg's in the mountains."

Morin, on Frederick Street, keeps a supply of excellent photographs of Indian and coolie types; Sellier, on Upper Prince Street, has fine views of scenery, and Casabon on Brunswick Square, owns a good collection of natural curiosities. All these are worth a visit.

If a call can be arranged at the Angostura bitters establishment of Dr. Siegert & Sons, it will be interesting, from the number of specimens of plants kept there.

Besides these tourist attractions, there is a variety of scene, a tone of society, and a diversity of things to do in Trinidad, that only Jamaica and Cuba of all the islands can equal. If any one has tried to lead a party of friends about in foreign lands, he will find the most difficult of his questions, "What shall we do next?" And, when one has become fairly well acquainted in Port-of-Spain, this *schwer Frage* answers itself.

ST. JOSEPH, TRINIDAD, March, 1891.

Chapter IX.

THE SPANISH MAIN.

THERE is but one way to reach the mainland of Venezuela from Trinidad, and so on down the Main, if the trip up the Orinoco be excepted; and as this in no way concerns us as exploring sanitarians, it will be spoken of later.

There are several lines of steamers that carry passengers to the Venezuelan ports, but the only one that is worth counting is the Royal Mail. Besides the occasional ships of the transatlantic fleet that run across, there is a regular service of what are called intercolonial boats, that are reliable, moderately fast, with a fair table and comfortable cabins. The only drawback has been the high rates they have charged, averaging ten dollars a day for short trips, and not much less for longer ones. But this season there is a change. Cook & Son have arranged tours starting from New York, following down the islands to Trinidad, by the steamers of the Quebec line, thence to La Guayra by the Royal Mail, and thence by the superb ships of the Red D Line home, via Curaçao. The trip may be reversed, as much time as needed taken at each island, and the whole at a remarkably low figure.

The time actually essential to do the journey properly, and not be too hurried, is six weeks; but it may be done in four. For most nervous Americans, this is a delightful

HARBOR ENTRANCES,

PUERTO CABELLO AND LA GUAYRA.

tour; embracing, as it does, a great variety of sea and shore, with frequent changes of scene, of people, language and food, and everywhere complete rest.

After arriving at Trinidad, where a stop of a few days will probably be enforced—for it is a rare thing for steamers of different lines to connect closely—the tourist who proposes to continue by the Main will do well if he goes to the office of the Royal Mail Company, at Port-of-Spain, and secures a comfortable cabin.

These steamers are built upon a totally different plan from American vessels. The cabins are large, commodious and scarcely furnished at all. The best of them are forward, where the cool breezes, which the steamer always faces, find their way to the sleeper in fresh purity, while occupants of the after state-rooms must manage to do with their atmosphere as it comes to them after playing about awhile among machinery and the boilers. As there is always a great demand for the few state-rooms forward the wisdom of my advice will be seen.

Another hint. Avoid taking passage by what are called the cargo boats, which do not have anything like as comfortable accommodations as the others. The run across to Puerto Cabello is a matter of a couple of days of pleasure sailing, and while there sufficient time is given to visit the pretty suburbs of Borburata and Sant Esteban, where worthy merchants of the city live in their quiet country houses, beneath the shadow of great mountains bearing primeval forests, in which tigers and other wild beasts dwell.

The little river of Sant Esteban sings merrily over pebbles at the bottom of a cool, dark ravine, eddying now and then into pools that are famous bathing places in the early morning.

About the streets of Borburata may be found gateways, with great walls, that open into gentlemen's gardens containing the most luxuriant wealth of tropical foliage that only dreams of these sunny lands have so far produced.

The market, too, is well worthy a visit. One finds there his first specimen of the famous cassava bread, in flat cakes three feet across and a quarter of an inch thick. He

NATIVE INDIAN HOME, PUERTO CABELLO.

carries home a loaf of bread much as he would a cart-wheel.

In the village of Sant Esteban are to be found specimens of feather flowers of exquisite colors and in excellent taste, made by native ladies. They may be purchased at reasonable prices, and while quite as good as those of Brazil, are much cheaper. Other curios or things to be bought, there are none.

In sea-port towns of the Spanish Main it is needful to be exceedingly cautious about nocturnal exposure. You may go about as much as you choose in the daytime, provided you are protected from direct sun rays, but night air is dangerous. It is much better to follow the example of the people who live there, and stay in-doors after sunset, and in bed after nine o'clock.

One may rise long before the sun, and find in the delicious morning air, with its cool freshness and novel rich perfumes, an ample recompense for unwonted labor in getting up so early.

From Puerto Cabello to La Guayra is six hours' sail, and is usually managed in the night, so as to give the ships all of daylight possible to load and unload cargo; but at La Guayra, which is the sea-port for Caracas, we must pause awhile, for it is within a mile of the Newport of Venezuela, pretty little Macuto, and, of course, we must go and see the swells of this country, who flock to the seashore in hot weather as do those of every land. A cab will drive us out and back for two dollars, and wait our pleasure there.

At Macuto are many handsome residences, and the best of them, when I was there last, was that of the President, Gen. Guzman Blanco. The streets are more peculiarly South American than in any town yet reached; narrow, well-shaded, bordered by single-storied houses with red tiled roofs. Glass windows there are none, and when the rainy season comes people close heavy wooden shutters, and thus defy the storm.

The bathing-beach at Macuto is not an especially attractive one, for sharks of the man-eating variety are so numerous that it has been found necessary to build a protection against them where people go into the water. This is a handsome round tower, some fifty feet out in the water, with separate divisions for men and women; and strangers are welcome to bathe upon payment of a small fee for towels.

From La Guayra to Caracas, which is the main point that we have come so far to visit, there is now an excellent railroad, thanks to the enterprise and public spirit of President Guzman Blanco. It climbs 3,400 feet in a distance of six miles, winding backward and forward in crevices in the rocks that have been dug with extreme difficulty, at a great cost of treasure and life. On the way up we passed through two or three dense flights of locusts, which were sufficiently numerous to give the impression of a cloud as they flew between ourselves and the sun. When they alighted on a tree it became instantly invisible, and there was nothing to be seen except a mass of these insects clinging to each other, hundreds deep, making a form of locusts somewhat resembling the original shape of the tree.

Sometimes, it is said, they alight upon the railway, impeding traffic, their bodies being so full of oil that when crushed by the wheels of the train the rails are greased enough to prevent progress.

Now and then the track skirts so closely to the edge of a tremendous precipice that one may look directly from the car windows into an abyss thousands of feet deep, at the bottom of which is a green plateau with specks here and there, which a glass resolves into men and moving teams.

The capital city of Venezuela lies in a basin surrounded by mountains, climbing up some seven thousand feet still higher than the plain on which it is built. It is laid out, this city of the Incas, upon a beautiful plain as level as a floor, richly watered by clear mountain streams that come

CARACAS.

foaming down the steeps, and supplied with the latest adjuncts of civilization in the way of electric lights, horse cars, and a daily press.

There are two excellent hotels, the Grand Hotel and Hotel America, both having English-speaking waiters, and charging moderate prices, say from two to three dollars a day. These are the only hotels that I know of in all South America where there are modern conveniences, as we call them.

The temperature of this plateau I found delightful, quite cool enough at night for double blankets on the bed, and a temperature of from 55° to 58°. At mid-day there was a rise, never exceeding 15°, with an average all day long of 68° F. So here, close to the equator, I found a temperate zone — one of exceedingly slight barometric variation, and that within a comfortable limit.

As might be expected, in such an ideal climate, there are no epidemic forms of disease. Occasionally yellow fever makes its appearance, brought by pilgrims from the coast; but it is years since an epidemic thereof has frightened the people. Colds and bronchial affections are probably common, not often, however, becoming dangerous. People suffering from one class of diseases must be cautioned against coming hither. These are affections of the heart, whether organic or functional. The great elevation of this mountain city produces a rarefaction of the air which is harmful to invalids of this class. Even well people may find themselves dizzy and confused in mind during the first few days of their stay at Caracas. Respiration is increased in rapidity, and the pulse-beat runs up. The American minister told me that it took him nearly a month to recover from this condition, and even after he had been a year in the city, he still suffered occasionally from ringing in the ears and slight dizziness. Therefore, it is better for the stranger within the gates to avoid violent exercise, and especially the use of stimulants. This latter is somewhat difficult advice to follow, for the hospitable people of the town are in the habit of drinking ardent spirits freely, and the first thing done to show courtesy to visitors is the production of an unlimited supply of drinks of all kinds.

There is probably no place in the world where cabs are so plentiful and cheap. Every one drives, from the President in his elegant landau, followed by a glittering bodyguard of horsemen, to the cook going to market,—all go on wheels. The price for a coach that will carry four is from two to three dollars a half-day, while single trips in an ordinary cab about town may be enjoyed for eight cents.

Artists will find in the beautiful scenery surrounding the city, a variety of subjects, which, taken with their novelty, will give ample occupation for any length of time. No more beautiful view exists than the one overlooking the road by which the Incas entered the town, with its beautiful double row of palms on either side of the bridge that crosses the river. It is unsurpassed in my memory of many lands.

If a tourist can so time his visit as to arrive in Caracas a few days before Shrove Tuesday, he will be in time to enter into the sports of the carnival, for which every Caraqueña is longing for weeks before it comes.

That morning begins with a free parade of all the city hacks and cabs, headed by the mayor and a brass band. The latter is usually in sections, which are sometimes a block or two apart, and by no means continue the same tune throughout; but this in no way interferes with the fun.

From the cathedral down the street called Carnival, there is a steady stream of carriages, loaded with bushels of small sweetmeats, miniature biscuits, flowers and an endless variety of light missiles.

Wide, Moorish windows are filled to the bars with pretty girls, who promptly open fire on the carriages as they pass, and a battle royal ensues. From every balcony, from windows, from passers on the street, there rains a steady stream of everything that can be thrown, and our carriage speedily began to look like a burned-out confectionery shop.

Venezuela draws its main revenue and its chief support from coffee culture, and a day or two cannot be spent more pleasantly than in studying the culture of this fragrant berry at some friend's estate.

Every one in this country talks coffee, raises coffee, deals in coffee, or owns coffee; but not a single soul appears to know how to make a cup of the beverage fit to drink, as Americans like it. It is burned quite black, thereby losing all aroma, and served as strong as it can be made, in which condition it is a nerve stimulant more potent than brandy, and its excessive constant use by all classes goes far to explain the nervous condition of the natives. Visitors are cautioned against following their example.

As a matter of course, at such an elevation in this tropical latitude, relative humidity is very great, and it is not an easy task to care for one's clothes. A pair of shoes that had not been worn for two or three days looked as if a garden had been started in them; and a lady friend told me of a silk costume that was ruined by mildew, because she left it unaired two days after wearing. In such a climate vegetation runs riot.

In Caracas valley alone there are over sixty varieties

A CUADRILLA PACKING COFFEE.

of orchids, and innumerable flowers and plants unknown to us, many of great beauty, others of deadly virulence; and the fauna is correspondingly rich.

In the territory between La Guayra and Caracas, scarcely

PATIO AT LA GUIA.

larger than New York city in area, may be found the best insect specimens of every zone.

Home life in Venezuela differs so much from our own that I venture to speak of a few things that seemed novel. After the first night's sleep ashore, morning brought with it an upland breeze, mountain odors of the balsamic eucalyptus, and a keen appetite, that only comes after rest and in health. The first meal was promptly served — desayuno, it is called — of coffee, with milk, delicious rolls, and cheese; and this is on the table at 7 o'clock.

Then comes an interval for walking, sketching, or making acquaintances, while the hostess is occupied with preparations for breakfast — an important affair.

This repast, called almuerzo, is served at 12. It begins with soup, runs up to half a dozen or more courses, finishes with sweets and black coffee, and leaves one in the best condition imaginable, quite ready for the siesta that follows a cigar.

In this noontide, human life is still, but the air is loud with sound. Thousands of insects, and many unknown birds, make the sunny day vocal, and from the mountain sides comes the whistle of a troupial or the scream of a macaw.

Then a long lounge upon the wide veranda, a pleasant drive through the cool, refreshing air over excellent roads, until lengthening shadows mark the approach of swift night-fall. Lamps are lighted, the table is again spread for dinner upon the verandah, where another hour or two is spent over a longer, more elaborate meal than the noon breakfast.

One of the gentlemen captured a lightning bug or cucullo, whose fiery plates shone brilliantly as he crawled about the table.

Madam's pet tree, an immense specimen of some sensitive plant, folded its leaves and went to sleep.

Delicious fragrance from flowers that only bloom in darkness came to us upon the cool breeze from distant hills, and strange constellations sparkled in the sky that grew black as night came on.

We dallied with coffee and cigar, and listened to sweet

voices talking Castilian, until there came to us a sense of absolute content that dwellers in Northern lands can never know.

A pleasant side trip may be made from Puerto Cabello to the inland city of Valencia, some sixty miles by rail. Here is an excellent hotel, a beautiful park filled with wonderful trees, splashing fountains and glittering lights, and near by the famous lake of Tara Yaca, the largest in the land.

Its people are intelligent and hospitable, and will always make it a pleasant place for those to visit who care to know more of the country than her sea-port cities can present.

It is hardly necessary to add that to obtain the best results from a visit to the Spanish Main one should speak Spanish, for no other language is used or known by the great mass of its population.

It is true that among the upper circles English and French are both spoken — the latter mostly; but wandering about the streets chatting with the people, or purchasing articles from the shops, at least some knowledge of the tongue that is native is necessary.

Throughout the country, with the sole exception of Caracas, everything is cheap. One can live in the way the people live for $2 a day; but I doubt if the majority of traveling Americans will grow fat upon such diet.

Their better plan is to retain rooms upon the ship, making such excursions as are possible while the steamer is in port.

From Venezuela the handsome ships of the "Red D Line" sail for home, calling at Curaçao, oldest of all the West India Islands, if indeed Curaçao may be classed among them.

THE START FROM CAMBUR.

Where the clear water of the Caribbean assumes its brightest, most transparent blue, lies this island, whose singular outlines, deep shining lagoons and landscapes, quaint with the architecture of by-gone days, interest every traveler whom fate leads to southern shores. One fancies on landing that he has been transported backward two hundred and fifty years, and has before him the city of New Amsterdam, as it was when Holland ruled Manhattan Island. Every house, and most of the figures might have been copied from ancient prints of old Dutch towns, and at church, when the minister came in wearing a black felt hat, and ceremoniously bowed to his audience before he mounted the winding stairs that led to his lofty pulpit, where he preached in fluent Dutch, the illusion grew until it seemed quite real.

The curios old streets are full of dark interiors, such as Rembrandt and Teniers have given us. Some of them are scarcely four feet wide. Into their depth the rays of a nearly vertical sun scarcely ever penetrates, and their best views are impossible to photography by reason of lack of light. But there are rare chances for painters in strange contrasts between the intense light that pervades the air, and the little dark, wide open shops where goldsmiths sit all day hammering out filigree work of gold, such as Etruscan jewelers once made; where now and then a shaft of fierce light cleaves its way through the darkness to a snowy turban, a crimson shawl, or the sparkling eyes of a naked baby. And such roofs, hanging gables, and picturesque blackness! Why, artists might spend months here, and find something new each day.

There are no wheeled vehicles, and tourists must walk if they choose to leave the single horse-car track. If by chance a friend is found who owns a carriage, the prettiest drive in the island is across to Hatto cave, where Captain Kidd, as story books say, once lived for many a day.

It is not necessary to have more than a slight acquaintance with Consul Smith to be assured of his hearty hospitality. His pretty steam yacht is always ready to carry a party of his countrymen about the lagoons, and his charming family are always glad to meet their countrywomen.

The island is especially healthy. During the winter months a steady average temperature of 70° F. prevails, with strong breezes that sweep the streets clean.

There are no epidemic diseases. Nights are cool and

THE GOVERNOR'S HOME, CURAÇAO.

quiet, and if there were a decent hotel, there is not a winter resort in the world where an invalid could be more comfortable or have a better chance to improve.

But so far there is no house for visitors, and tourists are compelled to remain on board ship, where they are made comfortable and are well cared for.

From Curaçao one may go to Maracaibo, about two hundred and fifty miles away, the journey lasting a week, and giving plenty of time to visit the wonderful homes of the lake dwellers, the only ones upon the western continent.

Before I left home, this far away city with musical name had been the chief point of attraction. No one seemed to know much about it — an excellent reason for going.

Every one with whom I talked warned me against trouble from terrible heat, awful accommodations, and the constant presence of yellow fever. As careful inquiry as I could make, negatived all these statements, and in care of Captain Reith and his Virginia darkey steward, no pleasanter journey could be made. Arriving, I found a city of some thirty-five thousand inhabitants, stretching its red-tiled roofs and many spires backward from the water till lost in distance of treeless cliffs or dark sand-hills. Essentially a tropical town, it is not, during the winter months, subject to tropical heat, a steady breeze keeping the thermometer down to 78 degrees while the sun was shining, and making nights cool enough for a blanket. When I wondered at this freshness, so different from the inferno of which I had been told, one of my new friends said that it was exceptional, that, usually the weather was much warmer, and in summer the heat was steadily over 95 degrees.

It seems curious that every place that I have visited in thirty years' travel has always presented exceptional weather. But as this was exceptionally good, no fault was found.

Maracaibo's streets are free from wheeled vehicles, except a few carts for hauling goods. A single livery stable has two or three carriages, which are rarely let, the reason being plain after a single drive about town and in the outskirts. Except along the docks and upon the Calle Derecho, (the street called Straight) driving is difficult, while outside of the town there are no roads at all.

When darkness comes, everybody goes to bed or otherwise disappears, and after eight o'clock the city is deserted. It is clean and healthful. Even in the narrow slums where Indians live, no offensive sights or smells are encountered, and diligent inquiry at hospitals established the fact that there had been no epidemic sickness for months.

There was not a case of fever of any kind, and the people looked robust and well.

Excellent water is supplied in profusion from a spring several miles away.

To the traveler and archæologist there is nothing more interesting than the town of Santa Rosas, where the lake dwellers have built their curious homes, and where the customs and manners of an age too far distant for history, remain in their primeval condition.

Even tradition cannot say when they began to live in these water houses.

They were there when the Spanish invaders passed them by as too poor for plunder, too insignificant for prey. No one knows where they came from. They cannot tell themselves, and all their history is lost, every tradition forgotten.

Even from Maracaibo it is not an easy matter to reach them, for their home is ten miles down the lake, and the only means of communication are those that the traveler finds for himself.

I spent an entire day at the village; obtained a number of photographs, some implements used in their daily lives, and a bundle of poisoned arrows with which they do their hunting.

Most of the young women are good looking. They are reared for sale, but on account of the general business depression, prices were low the chief said.

He offered me his daughter, a bright lass of sixteen, for twenty dollars, but traffic in human flesh is not a favorite business with Americans.

Visitors to Maracaibo, who are fortunate enough to be guests of Captain Reith, will have no difficulty in paying a visit to this wonderful village of the lake, and I regard a trip to the Spanish Main as incomplete which does not include a visit to its inland sea and its remarkable water village.

Sitting on the *Maracaibo's* deck, the evening when we sailed into Curaçao, homeward bound, a half dozen Venezuelans and the writer sat talking of travel, of pleasant acquaintances made and lost, and of the great improbability that all of us would ever see again the shores we had left a few hours before.

Sunset changed quickly to darkness as we ran into port, and, parting, I said to my new made friends. "Perhaps we may meet again in Venezuela, who knows."

They gravely answered, with uncovered heads, "Si Dios quiere, caballero."—" Sir, if God wills."

Chapter X.

COSTA RICA.

UNTIL a traveler leaves the Spanish Main, he hears nothing of the valuable and almost unknown health resorts of Central America. To most of our people, this country represents to the imagination little besides a wide expanse of primeval forest, perpetually baked by a tropical sun, seamed by a single mountain range, watered by a few insignificant rivers, and broken up into a number of independent states, which are inhabited by a savage and fierce race of people descended from the ancient Aztecs, and the Conquistadores who ravished from them their lands and made them a province of Spain instead. There are very few people among residents of the United States who could tell instantly if Central America, as a whole, is as large in area as Rhode Island or Texas, or who could say from what they remember of their geography just what part of the American continent it occupies. Nor is this to be wondered at. Her ports of entry, few in number and not readily accessible, have been credited with the constant presence of that deadliest enemy to northern life that the tropics contains, yellow fever. To this terrible disease northern imagination has ever attached an amount of fear greater than that perhaps of any other existing, and invalids, for whom these pages are more especially printed, do not care to go from bad to worse.

When, therefore, I commenced to write of the beautiful resorts of Central America the approach to which is quick, easy and safe, whose climate is perpetual spring, and where there are excellent hotels, competent physicians and mineral springs of extraordinary power, all under the supervision of a government republican in form and strongly favorable to Americans in every way, I expected that it would cause some surprise.

In the winter of 1888 and 1889 I paid a visit to the states of Central America with the object of studying her countries and their relative value as health resorts.

Besides a spirit of utilitarianism that prevails just now, there is a growing interest in many questions of a practical character, among which may be mentioned the early history of Central America and the monuments and traditions of its inhabitants, subjects well worth studying in vacation, if it be spent where the necessary conditions exist.

There are several ways of reaching the little republic that we are to visit, either from New York by the excellent steamers of the Atlas line, or from New Orleans by a line recently established. Other ships run from the Spanish Main, direct from La Guayra to Colon on the isthmus of Panama, where still others connect with the northern lines for Port Limon, the Gulf sea-port of Costa Rica.

The cost of these several journeys is about the same, amounting to $150.00 in round figures, each way. Once arrived at Port Limon, the rest of the way to the capital, San José, is at present traversed by a railway which has been built by an enterprising Yankee, Miner C. Keith, who practically controls the country.

When I made the journey two years ago, it was by mule with considerable difficulty and no small expense, to say

CRATER LAKE OF IRAZU.

nothing of the spice of occasional danger; and one needed a tolerably steady head and firm set of nerves to enjoy riding along brinks of precipices where a single false step would effectually prevent any further search for health.

At the sea-port there are no hotels, and it is best to remain on board ship until the morning when the train starts for the interior. As is the custom in all tropical lands, trains leave at an early hour; no inconvenience, however, when one becomes accustomed to going to bed early and rising with the birds.

In the heart of this beautiful republic, amongst the elevated and lovely valleys of the Andean chain, there is a sanitarium absolutely unique in advantages offered to health and pleasure seekers, boasting of sublime grandeur of scenery, and tranquil loveliness rarely surpassed. There are smiling valleys surrounded by the towering mountains of the Candelaria, the frowning volcanoes of Irazu and Turrialba, while from the earth hot springs pour out healing waters for whomsoever seeks their relief. Its atmosphere is cool and exhilarating, its extended forests abound with noble game, and its many lakes and streams contain plenty of fish. Besides which the region is full of important historic associations, while in monuments of the remote past and legends of the Central American Indians, it is unequalled.

Those who prefer a quiet, inexpensive and comfortable place where they can go dressed as they choose from day to day, and who can find pleasure in boating, fishing, and mountain exploring, or studying the customs and manners of a race of Indians whose manners and customs are as attractive as they are picturesque, will be sure to find what they seek in the charming valley of Cartago, where, at an elevation of 4,750 feet above the sea, with a temperature that does not vary 5° the entire year, say from 65° to 70° F. and hemmed in on all sides by the towering Andes, there is one of the loveliest spots in the world. It is thirteen miles by rail from San José, and the springs themselves are a mile and a half from Cartago. There is a picturesque village at the springs where a company has constructed a bath-house and hotel, with a tramway to connect the establishment with the main lines of rail, upon which cars will run to meet every train.

The view from the windows of the hotel comprises the whole valley of Cartago, with its old Spanish missions, and part of the valley of Orosi.

Guests can communicate with all parts of the world by telegraph.

Its climate is highly recommended for tuberculosis, as consumption is unknown in the country, and many cases brought here have been permanently cured.

In the surrounding mountains and forests are found more rare birds of beautiful plumage than elsewhere. All species of birds of Paradise, parrots and water fowls have made this their natural home.

For the botanist there are superb orchids, ferns, and air plants in variety not found elsewhere.

The coldest temperature observed throughout the year of 1889 was at 4 A. M. on the 11th of January, 59°. The highest was at 2 P. M. on the 30th of July, 71°.

During the months of January and February, not a drop of rain fell. During the months of March and April rain fell for seven days and eleven hours, with a total precipitation of ten millimetres. These figures show that the temperature of this favorite valley is that of perpetual spring, and I do not hesitate to recommend in the strongest possible way this favored spot as a sanitarium.

If tourists are fond of mountain climbing, they will be amply repaid by an ascent of the volcano of Irazu, and from its summit the Atlantic and Pacific oceans may be seen one hundred and sixty miles apart, and it is said to be the only place on the globe where this can be done. Its elevation is 12,000 feet.

People who do not like ascents, may readily find beautiful cataracts and rapids, among the best of which are the Falls of Paris, Falls of Colorado, and those of Orosi.

The temperature of the hot springs attached to the hotel at Agua Caliente are as follows:

No. 1,	131°
No. 2,	129°
No. 3,	138°
No. 4,	135°

And the following analysis has recently been made of their waters.

In each ounce there have been found two grains of solid matter, divided as follows:

Carbonate of Lime,	0.4
" " Magnesia,	.1
" " Iron,	.2
Chloride Soda and Potash,	.7
" Magnesia,	.2
Sulphate Lime,	.3
" Magnesia,	.1
Total grains,	2.

The gas which escapes with the water in considerable quantity is chiefly carbonic acid, and where the water cools,

PUBLIC PARK, SAN JOSE.

iron is precipitated, and at this temperature, 110°, contains 100 per cent. of gas, giving to the water a slightly metallic taste. These qualities make the springs valuable for convalescents from fever, and for all persons who are naturally of feeble constitution. They closely resemble the well-known waters of Aix la Chapelle and Baden.

Excursions may be made at any time to the capital city of San José, where thirty thousand people are living with all the comforts of modern progress and improvement.

There are macadamized streets, well-paved sidewalks, street cars, electric lights, handsome buildings and beautiful parks. There are several good hotels, two clubs, a public library, and a fair theatre, and English is more generally spoken than in any other Spanish American city on the continent.

Until last year the most prominent building was the beautiful cathedral, which, when it had just been finished at enormous expense, was almost totally destroyed by an earthquake.

While speaking of this undesirable accompaniment to a residence in Costa Rica, I may say that the shocks that are common are exceedingly slight, and that while I was in the country three or four were said to have occurred that I knew nothing of until informed by native friends. It is exceedingly rare that any harm is done to life or limb, and the shock that did so much damage to the cathedral building was the first of any severity that had occurred for years.

Every Sunday evening a military band plays in front of the President's residence, and the feature is one of great interest to strangers.

I copy the following from an article in *Harper's Magazine*, written thirty years ago, which is as true to-day as it was then:

"The narrow street is crowded with listening groups, surrounding the musicians standing at their music desks, whose lanterns pierce the shadows, reaching groups of ladies listening at the door-ways, each one smoking a cigarette; lighting up a scrawny, black sentinel, leaning at a door-post of the President's house, rubbing one bare foot against the other; showing the white-washed wall behind him, with a yellow candle in a glass case suspended from the ceiling, and an officer in white trowsers and gold-laced cap, who was just returning in-doors from an inspection of the crowd outside."

This was in January, and as we returned to our hotel at about midnight, and found not the slightest trace of dampness upon our thin clothes and uncovered heads, and went to bed in a room with open windows, where my thermometer marked 62°, the conclusion that we came to was, that Costa Rica was an excellent place to visit. It is more than I can say of other states of Central America. They appear to be at present in a condition of revolution, and it is not comfortable nor safe for an American to visit either Guatemala or San Salvador while the memory of the late American Minister remains, as it does to-day, a shameful thing in the minds of the natives and a disgrace to the administration that made him an American representative.

Expenses of all kinds are higher in Central America than in any of the West India islands.

Food supplies, with the exception of fruit and beef, are all imported from far away, by means of a small and expensive line of steamers, and hotel bills are necessarily high.

At the springs a tourist may live for about three dollars a day, at the capital for about four dollars, and everything in the way of clothing is dear. Cab fare, or mule hire,

SILVER MINING IN COSTA RICA.

which usually replaces the cab in Central America, is also high on account of the difficulty of procuring wheeled vehicles from Europe or the United States, the lack of skilled mechanics to keep them in order, and a scarcity of animals. Horses, although small, are cheap, active and wiry, and may be depended upon to do good work for long distances. They may be hired for about two dollars a day.

Guides are very necessary through the forests and among the mountain ravines, and in common with all forms of service, they are cheap and reliable. A good peon charges from thirty to fifty cents a day, and finds himself. He also finds anything and everything that is lying around loose, which is more than the owner ever does afterward. Clothing is about the same as we wear in summer, the cool nights frequently making light wraps comfortable.

PORT LIMON, COSTA RICA, 1890.

Chapter XI.

JAMAICA

HAZY CLOUDS hung over the mountains of Cuba as they faded in Northern distance to mingle with horizon sky, while from the deck there grew from southern sea a chain of lofty hills that mark the black republic of Haiti. A little to the west another range of peaks sharply defined itself against reddening sunset clouds, and we were studying first impressions of the Blue Mountains of Jamaica.

Before my visit there, I was surprised to learn how meagre were sources of information concerning the land. Except a few newspaper letters, there was nothing of a general or popular style, and it therefore gives me especial pleasure to present to Americans this charming island, as almost *terra incognito*.

At best it is known as a West Indian island where oranges grow, and when I began preparations for the trip I was asked what language was spoken there more than once.

Between the United States and this island there are many bonds of mutual like and interest, growing stronger of late by reason of increase of acquaintance and a waxing commercial intercourse. More frequent means of communication have been established, more Americans have gone there to invest money and live, and this is one of the few West Indian islands were there are distinctively American hotels.

SPRINGFIELD VILLA.

Our people do not find the houses at Constant Spring or Myrtle Bank different in arrangement or management from those in the Adirondacks or Florida, and may engage rooms in advance as at home. The railways are owned and run by an American company, and Yankee farmers have exchanged the cultivation of Massachusetts potato fields for that of Jamaica banana orchards, to the great and manifest improvement of their exchequer.

With this better knowledge of each other, the two countries, for, like most progressive British colonies, Jamaica holds claim to separate existence, there has grown up a cordial amity pleasant to learn of—more pleasant to experience.

It is but a generation since the sugar planters of Jamaica were famous the world wide for exceeding hospitality. Their regal incomes were spent with generosity as lavish as the soil that provided them, and merely to be a stranger in those days was to be certain of such entertainment as only honored and expected guests could command in other lands.

With lessening value for their product came smaller means to expend, and most of the old magnificence is gone except in story. But the same generous hearts remain to make the most of minished incomes, and there is to-day needed only one proper letter of introduction to make a wandering stranger free of every guild in Jamaica.

He is passed on from home to home, sumptuously fed and lodged and so kindly made one of the family, that it is difficult to part with such big-hearted friends when the hour comes, and there is always afterward in his heart a large regard for Jamaica and her noble people, and anxious desire to have a chance to reciprocate their hospitality.

Its advantages to health-seeking tourists are many and peculiar, and they will be fully described in this chapter. Not least among them is the fact that it may be reached in four days from New York by several lines of steamers, the best of which is the Atlas. Who sails on the Adirondack will have a safe and comfortable voyage. Then there are the morning public telegrams and constant arrivals of strangers from all parts, for Kingston is a great port of call, and almost daily sailings for some American port. All these help to make Jamaica popular.

For it is not enough to be acquainted with tables of humidity, of heat or of air pressure; it is quite necessary that travelers should know something of the locality they choose to visit and its specialties, since it is not the presence or absence of great things that makes up the list of advantages of one place over another to a tourist, especially if he chance to be an exiled invalid.

It is the many mickles that make the muckle, each small enough by itself, perhaps, but adding fast to the sum total of what makes a residence or a visit in a strange place pleasant.

It is better to know what society one can get into and how natives amuse themselves, than to fret about the heat, the difficulty of finding home dishes at tables, the annoyance of crowds of negroes everywhere, and the many other points of difference that are not always agreeable. To be a good traveler is indeed a rare gift, and bestowed only upon those whom the gods delight to honor; but there are few who cannot manage to approximate to so lofty an ideal, if they will sedulously cultivate contentment of mind and cheerfulness of spirit, together with a temper that nothing shall ruffle, and a stomach too strong for dyspepsia. With these qualifications taken for granted, we may inquire:

Are hotels comfortable and not too dear?

Can one find in the chosen resort such privileges of church, libraries and lounging places as he is accustomed to, or must he depend entirely upon his letters of introduction and the natural attractions? Is there a good club house, where an hour may be whiled away pleasantly, the latest news received and the best men in town met? These are not great things, truly, but they make up a large part of a traveler's comfort, if he is to remain in one place more than a day or two, and it is almost impossible to know of their existence except from some one who has been there.

There are several excellent hotels in Kingston, and a number of respectable boarding houses. The exposition year was naturally a busy one for all these houses, and they were well tried. The Park Place and Sonnenschein's are excellent native inns, where a traveler may be perfectly comfortable at the regular rate, $2.00 a day, no extras. Constant Spring and Myrtle Bank are under American management, with home prices and ways. The former is a couple of miles out of town, with a slow dusty tramway to take, the latter in a charming location in Kingston, where one may lounge through hot mid-day under palms or other shade and enjoy fresh sea breezes coming straight off the bay.

As to climate ranges, the following table will speak more authoritatively than my limited experience can do.

It is taken from the hand-book of Jamaica, 1888-9, and is from the pen of Maxwell Hall, M. A., F. R. A. S. The readings of the barometer and thermometers are taken at 7 A. M. and 3 P. M., local mean time, and have been corrected to Kew standard; the dew point has been deduced from dry and wet bulbs by means of Glaisher's factors, and every care has been taken to insure accuracy.

KINGSTON, JAMAICA, MEAN RESULTS FOR 1887—ELEVATION SIXTY FEET—MEANS FOR MONTHS.

MONTHS.	TEMPERATURE		DEW POINT.		HUMIDITY.		REMARKS.
	7 A.M.	3 P.M.	7 A.M.	3 P.M.	7 A.M.	3 A.M.	
January	68.7°	82.4°	65.2°	70.5°	89	68	Fair, slight earthquake 9th
February	68.6	81.9	64.2	67.6	77	63	Fine.
March	70.6	81.7	63.2	66.6	77	69	Fine.
April	75.7	81.2	67.8	71.0	77	70	Fair, with showers.
May	78.9	83.0	69.8	71.5	74	69	Fair, rainy season 15th.
June	79.3	84.0	70.3	72.1	74	68	Fair, with showers.
July	79.9	86.0	69.9	73.8	74	66	Fair, rain at end of month
August	77.6	84.0	71.1	74.2	81	74	Fair, afternoon showers.
September	77.7	85.0	71.3	74.2	79	68	Cloudy, earthquake 23d.
October	75.7	82.0	70.3	73.4	84	74	Rain first half, fair last.
November	74.0	84.0	68.6	73.3	84	71	Fair, with northers.
December	69.1	83.0	63.5	70.4	83	55	Fine.
Mean	74.6	83.4	68.0	71.6	80	69	

Sloan's Natural History of Jamaica, says: " Generally speaking, the two great rainy seasons are in May and October." During the winter months of December, January and February, and March, which is worse than either of the others at home, the weather is continuously fine. I was on the island thirty days during my last visit and saw but one slight shower, which did not extend over a half mile of area, and lasted fifteen minutes.

It will be seen from the above table that the variation of temperature for four months is barely five degrees, dew point and humidity about the same, and barometric pressure, which I have omitted, steady at 30 inches. This presents, I believe, as favorable a record as can be shown, and I leave the figures to speak for themselves.

The first consideration in thinking of any particular place as a winter home is, what it is especially beneficial for, and who would be likely to lose ground if sent there. My own stay was too short to learn, and I answer in the words of my friend, Dr. J. C. Phillippo, who has been a leading physician of the island for twenty-five or more years.

"Jamaica offers a great variety of climate, being in this respect unique among the West India islands. Invalids with dyspepsia and nervous diseases will scarcely improve in upland ranges, doing well in Kingston, while the entire island is extremely valuable in bronchial affections, pulmonary diseases, and all forms of rheumatism. There are valuable saline, sulphurous and chalybeate springs, which are among the most effective in the world. There is no necessity to watch winds, as the island is in about the middle of the trades, and has no strong gales in winter months. In the lowlands, temperature varies a few degrees from 80 as a maximum, but may be brought to any desired coolness by ascent of mountain sides. One always knows when rains are coming, their advance guard being visible at a distance upon the mountains, giving time to seek shelter, and showers always follow regular courses, reaching certain points at certain times. There is a constant unvarying high temperature, and yellow fever is almost a myth."

I learned also from Surgeon-General Morse, C. B., and Dr. Frank N. Saunders, Chief Medical Officer of the General Hospital, that many cases of cure of advanced consumption are on record and that they consider the island climate particularly valuable in lung diseases generally.

From Kingston to Porus, on the way to the mountain village of Mandeville, one goes by train for $1.25, thence taking a carriage the rest of the way, which will carry two passengers and the luggage for $2.25. Besides Brook's Hotel, there are two remarkably comfortable houses, Mrs. Roy's and Mrs. Halliday's, where a traveler will be sure to have home care and comforts at moderate rates. As there is considerable demand for rooms at Mandeville, arrangements should be made by wire or post before going up.

For a week or two, or for a season, the traveler may spend his time in a most delightful way there, and eat the famous mountain oranges, which I consider the finest in the world. He may stroll in flower gardens amongst unknown blossoms; may sketch or paint wide landscapes of tropical beauty; may visit the club-house, where tennis and cricket are favorite games; or he may sit upon his piazza after a good dinner and watch the coming of the glory of a tropical sunset far up among the hills. These are sufficient occupations for most people, plus getting well as quickly as possible, and improvement comes with rapidity.

Americans need carry no other money than their own. What goes in New York is good there and better further south. Eagles and greenbacks are exchanged at the Atlas Line office at par, or are freely taken at hotels and shops.

Jamaica has, what is especially valuable in a sanitary point of view, medicinal baths. There is no place in the world that combines the advantages of a climate like this with so many valuable spring and river baths as this charming island. Invalids with dyspepsia and nervous diseases will do better in Kingston than in the upland ranges; while the entire island is extremely valuable in bronchial affections, pulmonary disease, and all forms of rheumatism.

Let me quote again my friend, Dr. Phillippo. In his

book "*The Mineral Springs of Jamaica*" he calls attention to "the bath of St. Thomas the Apostle; the Jamaica Spa, and the Milk River bath." To which I add the Rock Pool, at Port Henderson. Speaking of the first one, he says the water is "unusually light, sparkling when received into a glass, fermenting slightly with acids, turns silver black, and seems specially charged with volatile products. It restores the appetite and natural action of the bowels, invigorates circulation, cleanses the urinary passages, strengthens the nerves, and seldom fails to give one an easy sleep at night. Its continued use enlivens the spirits, and sometimes produces almost the effect of inebriation. These springs may be ranked as hot thermic, sodic, calcic waters, having a temperature of 120° to 130° F."

Jamaica Spa lies among the mountains of Port Royal, at an elevation of about 3,500 feet above the sea level, and is to be reached by saddle animals at a distance of three hours from Kingston. The springs have a temperature of 66°, with clear, colorless water that leaves a red deposit in the spring and along the course of its discharge. They contain sulphates of iron, lime, magnesia, and alum, in considerable quantities, are strongly chalybeate, astringent to taste, and only need development to make them very valuable.

Milk River baths belong to the Government. In their circulars the directors say that the institution will furnish visitors with everything but food, for forty cents a day; and the matron will supply the latter at one dollar per day. They are readily accessible by steamer direct, or by rail and comfortable carriage.

He says: "I remember that an old surveyor whose joints were bent and distorted with rheumatism, went away in a totally helpless state to this spring, and returned in two or three weeks riding gaily on horseback, ready to set about his arduous labor. I have seen people who had been weeks in bed with acute rheumatism, sent down in carriages, taken into the bath in a chair, who have been able after three or four baths to walk up and down twenty or thirty steep stone steps with ease and comfort, and permanently cured. A well-known physician was there suffering with gout, and after three days was able to go out and dine with a friend at a distance. The proper months to spend at Milk River are January, March, and April."

In speaking of this island and its many charms, I am fain to take time. Its great area, its attractive and varied scenery, its many and growing industries — and its high rank as a sanitarium, deserve a careful study. Naturally, this cannot be exhaustive in a work like this; but its most interesting and enjoyable points demand and are to receive more care than even the largest of our chain of islands, Cuba the Queen.

Steamers enter Kingston harbor through a narrow passage guarded by "Apostles" fort; half an hour brought the city close at hand, and in a few minutes we were ashore among its low-lying streets, open drains, fire-scarred buildings and multitudinous negroes. There were narrow streets bordered by brick walls opening by iron gates to gardens gay with flowers, fountains and singing birds, or by heavy doors to scenes of dismal poverty that no sunbeams could lighten; handsome residences far back from dusty roadways, showing white through shade of palms and parasites; hovels of low degree and dark with grime, and wide, open spaces alternating.

We had seen similar pictures in other cities of our sunny islands, but they had no such background as those of Kingston. Scarcely farther away than suburban huts, rose in bold relief the steep sides and rain-scarred cliffs of the famous Blue Mountains, whose singular coloring, equally noticeable by day or moonlight, set the low city forward in the view. Against this azure mass, darkening in tint where gorges cut deep or clearing as projecting crags come nearer, fan-like palm tops and white spires of the town are drawn in sharp lines like an etching, with half tones rare in Nature's landscape hereabout.

Fleecy clouds that gathered here and there in sepia masses threatening rain without fulfilment of their promise, cut in twain the mountains and brought them still more sharply forward. From my charming home at Mona, those tranquil hills seemed close at hand, though still a league away, so pure was this wonderful atmosphere.

Some four thousand feet aloft, the camp of Newcastle clung to the mountain side, its white walls shining like tents in the sunlight, and its boundary lines showing on the slope as if drawn upon a map. Soldiers up there can only walk at an angle, and have no other exercise; but the climate is delicious, so cool that blankets are grateful at night and so even that fruit, vegetables and flowers grow all the year round. At varying heights, these mountains hold many pretty villages, where palms and peaches, bananas and strawberries, coffee flowers and geraniums flourish side by side, and a Northerner may have his native cool air with tropical scenery about him.

To see Jamaica best, a trip should be made around the island in the Atlas coasting steamer, which sails on exact time, is comfortable and takes a week for the trip. Weather is always fine, and meals may be eaten on deck, while Capt. Walker has been so long about the island that he is a perfect mine of information. Amateur photographers will find an enthusiastic devotee to the art in the purser, whose cabin is a darkroom at pleasure.

When I made the journey, there was on board the steamer from Kingston to Savanna-la-Mar, an English officer on an inspection tour, a genial gentlemen and capital story teller. He had served for many years in South Africa, where he had unconsciously posed for Rider Haggard's hero picture in "Jess."

All the charming evening we sat listening to reminiscences of Haggard and his characters. He had known Allen Quatermain well as a daring English hunter named Rogers, who spent months among the mountains where King Solomon's mines were said to be, and returned to town to spend all his earnings in wild dissipation. Haggard's local studies are true to life, said the captain, and most incidents told in his marvelous tales are either copies of popular legends widely believed in South Africa, or founded thereon with small addition.

Jess and her sister he knew well as Boer girls of moderate beauty, but endowed with unflinching courage. As we listened, there came this story of a daring feat by Jess, so creditable to woman's wit and woman's pluck, that it is well worth place on any page.

During the Boer war in the Transvaal, our captain was placed in command of a fortress which protected some six hundred women and children from murder and worse, with a single company of British soldiers for garrison. Around the earthen walls, sufficient protection against an enemy without artillery, between them and the nearest English force, lay many miles of rocky and desolate country swarming with savage foes, who, occupied with more important matters, had thus far refrained from deliberate siege of the little fort. Days passed and weeks, with no greater casualty than an occasional victim among the women, whose curiosity tempted them to climb the parapet to look out and so to meet death from a watchful Boer.

This was finally stopped by an order to the sentries to to pull the women off the wall feet first, and modesty conquered curiosity.

They had plenty of water from a well in the fort; but, as weeks passed, food grew scarce, starvation stared them in the face, and still the fierce foe beleagured them closely. At last there was but one thing left, word must be sent for help and that at once. But how? In every direction the country was traversed by bands of savage Boers, more bloodthirsty and relentless than even Zulus, and their fort was closely watched. He called for volunteers among the men, but none responded. Then Jess stepped forward and said, "Give me the message, captain, I will try to get it through. I know the country well, am native Boer; and, although my father and my brothers would murder me with awful tortures if I should be discovered, my way will be best, I am sure. Only write your message upon a metal surface and I'll hide it in my own way."

So a bullet was hammered flat, and upon its smoothness the captain scratched, "Come to our rescue, we are starving." Meanwhile, Jess procured some native salve used to produce blisters among her tribe, bared her shapely bosom and soon produced upon it a sore place large enough to conceal beneath the raised skin the bit of lead bearing all their lives. Here she hid the message, drew her clothing over it, and as nightfall came started on her perilous journey. Hardly had she gone a mile when quick-eyed sentinels spied and instantly captured her. When taken to the chief, she told her story of escape from the fortress as a prisoner, proved her Boer nativity, and submitted her entire person to a vigorous search for any suspicious sign of falsehood, which discovered, would have consigned her to speedy death by torture too terrible to name. But all went well, and her savage captors did not dream that beneath that angry sore upon her breast lay the message that they were seeking. They gave her her liberty, a pass, her clothing, and a horse, and told her to go to her home, and stay there. Making a wide detour she reached the English lines safely, delivered the leaden message to the commander, who promptly sent a force with provisions to the fort, and thus the brave girl saved her sisters. After the war closed, continued the captain, Jess disappeared from notice, probably as wife to one of her countrymen, who certainly won a brave lassie.

At last our steamer came along, and we were off for Lucea, of which both memory and camera have preserved charming souvenirs. As we swept around a headland and entered the harbor by a narrow gateway, the land gave way right and left in semi-circular sweep to form a circular port of perfect kind and sparkling beauty, upon whose western shore, sharply sloping down from mountains, nestled among palms and flowering trees, the quaintest, prettiest little white-walled town of all Jamaica. An easy ascent led to a clean-cut, stately little church, whose outlines are worth preserving.

The genial rector driving past took stock of a stranger in his domain, and with hearty cordial salutation, placed himself at my disposal.

"What can I do for you, sir?" he courteously asked.

"Will you go up to the church and see what it is like inside, or will you care to go with me and drive about, as I am off upon a school visit some miles away?"

But time would permit of neither, and when I learned how busy a man the rector was, with a variety of offices and none too much leisure, the decison was felt to be a wise one.

Like many other places in the islands, Lucea gives evidence of former wealth, now departed. I have a photo of a court-house of sufficient size to hold law givers for a hundred thousand people, that shows signs of sad neglect, and is flanked by a ruined arch of cut masonry, whose lights and shadows in white sunlight were artistic in the extreme, but not evincing prosperity. Streets made curves of many curvatures, and each turn was attractive, as it was almost sure to give a shining bit of bay to close perspective, while up through each a strong northern sea-breeze swept all day long. Although mercury marked 82° in the shade, no sensation of discomfort was felt, even while small exertion made every skin pore a miniature fountain, and clothing clung closely to one's person.

Everywhere the great preponderance of black blood showed plainly. To each white face, a dozen colored were encountered, and even the few Caucasians met with were so tanned by long exposure to this steady sun glare, that their skins lacked little of their neighbors' swarthiness. The question here and everywhere in Jamaica is, "Who is pure white?" Many generations of miscegenation have produced a distinct race, called "brown people," some of whom are blondes of pure type, occupying prominent positions in state and society circles, and jealous to the last extreme of their blood.

A ludicrous incident that occurred while I was in Kingston will illustrate this touchiness, and as actual fact, is worth recording. A gentleman who had been accorded hospitality by the Jamaica Club for a night, leaving early in the morning sought the black steward of the club who had assigned him to a room the night before, to pay his bill. Unable to find him, unacquainted with the place, he asked a gentleman taking early coffee. "Where shall I find the colored man who runs this club?" It so happened that the secretary who really was manager, chanced to have in his descent some distance back a little tint of color; and although perfectly white and a gentleman of education and leisure, partook of the absurd jealousy of race that is in universal force.

For a joke, the member of whom the question was asked repeated it, neglecting to add that the black steward was the person in question. The secretary flew into a passion, sat down and wrote to the member who had put the stranger up, demanding the latter's expulsion and criticising his nomination as improper. Of course, the true statement then came and the foolish secretary was compelled to apologize ; but it will be long before he loses the nickname "the colored man who runs the club."

Among these brown people are examples of superb physical development, mental acumen and personal beauty. Nowhere have I seen prettier women than some of the fair communicants of the parish church at Kingston, whose black eyes, clear brown complexion and round figures, with charming faces destitute of any negro cast, made them very attractive. Among the men are instances of great energy, business capacity and wealth, and despising as they do every allusion to any negro origin, they form a separate body of some hundred thousand souls, who may be counted upon to stand by the whites, should any race troubles arise.

But to return to our journey. From Lucea, splendid roads run east and west along the coast, and one toward the interior, whereby the pens, as Jamaican country homes are universally termed, are reached. I saw some splendid specimens of cattle hereabouts, and was told that no finer animals were raised in any country. Montego Bay came next and although not as valuable as a harbor as the one just left behind, it presented a beautiful appearance from the sea and was almost as pretty ashore. The town has a population of about five thousand souls, a large and increasing commerce and the only hotel worthy the name in the island outside of Kingston.

So far as location goes, perched upon a hill several hundred feet above the sea, facing to the north and commanding a series of beautiful sea and landscapes, with large airy rooms of pleasant aspect, I saw no public place in Jamaica so attractive for a prolonged visit. I found half a dozen New Englanders domesticated there, who seemed as happy as possible and spoke highly of their pleasant home. They were paying seven dollars a week for rooms and board, cheap enough surely. Home society in Montego Bay is cultivated and hospitable. At an evening spent with new made friends, it would not be fair to call those warm-hearted hosts of mine mere acquaintances, I met a dozen ladies and gentleman of intelligence and refinement in whose company music and conversation passed away the hours until midnight with astonishing speed. Most of them had been educated in the "States" as they called our country, and were enthusiastic admirers of the republic. Indeed, I found this sentiment of attachment to America wide spread and deep rooted. Said one prominent gentleman to me, "although a native or Great Britain, with fond love for my native land, I am convinced that the future prosperity of Jamaica lies in American, not English hands. Our geographical position, our commerce and our natural tendencies all combine to draw us toward the great republic: and I believe that a large majority of our people would cheerfully vote for annexation to your country." "Yes," I replied, "it is certain that it would be best for you, but the United States cannot burden itself with any sharply defined territory that is overrun with blacks. Precisely the same aid would be needed from us that England now refuses to extend to you, and there are too many miles of our own domain yet lying wild to make acquisition of your island either popular or politic. Some day in the distant future you will gravitate to the stars and stripes like Canada and Mexico, but it must be in natural course of events and cannot be brought about by politicians. "Well," said he, "I do not agree; it may be hastened at least."

Many of the island names bear evidence of Spanish possession and are almost the only traces to be found of the old time conquistadores, the most rigid search failing to reveal any history or document left by them. Even their priests who were careful to preserve records of every occurrence upon the Main so close at hand, seem to have totally neglected their duty in Jamaica during the hundred and fifty years of their occupation, and among the most ancient records there are none of Castilian origin. In the library of the Jamaica Institute I found some curious old volumes in English, depicting with pen and pencil Spanish atrocities upon harmless natives, and the retaliatory tortures inflicted by stout buccaneers whenever they took a hand in the game, but nothing more. It seems singular that among a race so fond of writing as Spanish ecclesiastics proved themselves elsewhere, they have entirely lost this century and a half, but it is possible that something of the kind may still exist in Madrid, where many documents concerning "Nueva España" still remain.

Montego Bay, for example, was called by Columbus and his men, "Puerto del Manteca," "Butter Harbor," because it was in their day a great emporium for that useful article. In like manner the musical "Rio Agua-alta" has been fused into "Wag Water River," an odd corruption.

Falmouth comes next, another open roadstead, partly protected from northerly gales by a coral reef called Bush Key. In Jamaica's palmy days, the planters of those good old times must have thought that their Pactolean stream would never run dry, and they built as they felt. There is a splendid court house, three stories high and façade of Corinthian columns, with a cool arcade of stone arches, flights of broad marble steps, spacious rooms for all sorts of officers, and a grand banqueting hall or ball room of the last century. It was built to stay, too; and, although the lavish expenditure that erected it is no longer possible, it is in fairly good repair. In the great hall are full length portraits of bygone magnates, and only a slight effort of imagination was needed to people its smooth floor with gay dancers, clad in costumes of a past age.

A little inland is the Spaniard's hidden gold mine. Near the village of Martha Brae, the legend says, was the olden city of Metilla, where many rich Castilians once lived. Constantly harried by buccaneers and no less dreadful filibusters, they had long been in the habit of burying their wealth as the only sure means of hiding it. When they were finally driven from the island, departure was so precipitate that there was no time to unearth the treasure, which remained behind, and still lies concealed "the secret gold mine." Many careful searches have been made, but the fortunate finder has not yet appeared.

Beautiful views of mountain and river scenery abound in this neighborhood, but there are few of sufficient local color to make them valuable. For the most part, they are such as are readily found in any tropical island where mountain ranges are, and are thus less valuable.

Dry Harbor in the parish of St. Ann's, obtains its name from the total lack of fresh water supply other than rain. Yet along its sandy shores groves of cocoa palms and logwood flourish luxuriantly, and in the middle of the dry season, no one would suspect how scarce fresh water is. I strongly suspect that energy enough to sink wells to a moderate depth would be promptly rewarded.

Columbus landed here when he discovered Jamaica, and expressed his delight at the beauty of the landscape before him.

Our thoughtful captain had wired to have carriages ready for a drive to Brown's Town, a thriving village a dozen miles inland, and we were promptly on hand. It was a delightful little trip. Slowly climbing along a fine road the way wound in and out through rocky defiles and dense tropical jungle, where delicious coolness of thick shade was made fragrant by sweet odors from many unknown flowering plants that covered the banks on either side. Sudden turns gave pictures of deep mountain gorges, whose sides were shadowed with darkest green, opening as by a telescope, upon a sheet of silver sea far below. Still higher, we come upon a vale whose perfect loveliness drew from all expressions of delight.

A little farther we came to groves of pimento trees, the allspice of the North, whose cultivation is a great industry at St. Ann's. The tree is a graceful copy of a Northern shell bark, or hickory tree, with smaller leaves and fragrant, white, star-shaped flowers. Beneath their shade, herds of handsome cattle grazed contentedly, and added much to the picture.

Only one drawback exists to tramping in Jamaica, but a serious one. Every foot of surface is infested by red ticks, known here as "bête rouge," a villainous insect about as big as a pin's point, that covers your skin and clothing in an instant after you land in grass, proceeds to bury himself with promptitude and success, and starts a sore that itches and burns like fire. After half a dozen have been dug out with a knife or needle, one grows cautious and confines his walk to cleared paths. Women's skirts collect them in swarms, and so ladies have a fair excuse for not walking in the country. There is a larger breed that makes deeper sores, called chigoes, or familiarly jiggers; but these are rare, and I did not see a single specimen during my stay.

No part of Jamaica is so rich in scenic beauty as St. Ann's. From the sea, as we sailed along its coast, thick groves of dense verdure ascended steep mountain sides that dipped their feet into warm wash of Caribbean, and across the water there came to the ship sweet scents of orange flowers, jasmine, and strange plants. From fastnesses far up cliff sides, sprang foaming, brawling brooks that need but a few hours rain to make them respectable rivers, and rain falls measuring three or four inches in an hour are not unheard of. Then these streams that now dance in harmless glee over their mossy paths, and add their foamy lace to the picture that we never cease to admire, become raging torrents, terrible engines of destruction, before whose great power all obstacles that lie in their downward rush to the sea are destroyed.

Columbus called St. Ann's bay, "Santa Gloria," and the pretty little town with its picturesque church and trim iron market-house, was a favorite home of the Spaniards. A little to the west they built their first capital, "Sevilla d'Oro," under the patronage of the first Spanish governor, who came to the island in 1509, bearing commission from Don Diego Columbus.

Hereditary viceroy of the New World, Don Juan d'Esquivel, being a noble of wealth and cultivated taste, soon made his capital home so charming, that it took rank above any Spanish city that has since followed it. There were built in his time, a fine theatre, superb palaces, a monastery and a cathedral, whose pavement alone measured two miles in length. But before long hardy natives, incensed by foreign oppression or tempted by rich display, fell upon the courtiers of Golden Seville and exterminated them, which caused the capital to be moved to Spanish town in the interior, which had been settled nine years before the other. Here it would still be, but for a mistaken governor, named Grant, who moved the seat of government to Kingston, where it is at the mercy of any attacking fleet in case of war. All of St. Ann's is rich in romance and history. A little to the eastward of the town is a pretty cove, still bearing the name of Don Christopher. Here Columbus came at the close of his fourth and last voyage, tired and disgusted,—all his fleet gone but two small caravels,—and these so strained and leaky as to be unseaworthy, and drove them ashore upon the white sand of this little bay that will always keep his name.

Near by this spot is Roaring River Cascade through whose white water black rocks show in fantastic forms, and we amused ourselves finding our initials therein. Like shapes that come at fancy's call in bright embers at Hallowe'en, each found with ease what he sought. Close at hand in Shaw's Hall Estate, where the Castilian dynasty came to a close, and its final representative, Don Sasi, had hidden, in vain effort to escape pursuit of Cromwell's fierce fanatics. They hunted him down and he had just time to escape in a small boat from the curving beach near by when they were at his heels. But he carried his life to Cuba, and when the red and gold of Spain's banner disappeared in his little barque, Castilian reign in Jamaica was done, and the year of our Lord 1655 had come in.

Port Maria and Annatto Bay seem to be destitute of tradition or story; but a mournful group of natives who stood wistfully gazing seaward at a receding ship, interested me much, for I heard the word Obeah spoken two or three times among them, and hoped to get on track of the ancient religion of Jamaica which I knew to be practiced yet in a modified form. Not as in savage Haiti, where human sacrifices are regularly offered by Voudoo priests in defiance of law, and where cannibalism is upon the increase in this nineteenth century—but in a mild and bloodless way. Yet Obi-ism, serpent worship, stills exists in the island, and at Port Maria, I found a clue that later gave me good results. Among the group of sad darkies on the wharf was a mother, whose girl had sailed away, cursed by the district Obeah man. After her departure, a charm was found in her vacant room; a little roll that held a tooth, a bit of glass and a few hairs,—enough to insure some mortal injury to the absent one, hence those tears. Judicious expenditure of coin and coaxing induced the boy who told me this story to bring an Obeah man to my hotel, where we had a pow-wow. He told me that he was a great "shadow catcher," and that when once he had captured a person's intangible image, his life and property were ever afterward at his disposal for good or ill.

With much looking about for listeners and apparent fear of detection, he confided to my sworn secrecy the fact that only two nights before, he had held incantation rites which he thus described. Only I cannot pretend to render his dialect and have my notes to transcribe from. "I went into the woods, master, back of Half-Way Tree, with another Obeah man, and we dug a hole for a grave. Then I took a chicken, cut his head off, caught the blood in the grave and said six, seven, nine prayers. Then I bring the blood back to town and sell it to a man for two pound, and dis man find his enemy soon dead. He catch him shadow."

I tried for an hour to get him to promise another midnight trip, when I proposed to take a camera and magnesium flash along; but no persuasion and no sum at my command had the smallest influence and he seemed frightened at having revealed so much. I learned from a police inspector, that fear of Obeah and belief in his power is almost beyond conception. Even in a court room, under oath, a negro will obstinately keep silence if a priest of the faith has commanded him. If Obeah is set for a man, as they call those nocturnal rites, he promptly becomes useless from fear, paralyzed, and sits down to wait his doom. Nor do these priests confine their worship to one god; they are often, I was told, ministers in charge of Christian chapels and country congregations over whom they thus exercise double influence. From a book on Jamaica customs that I came across, the following dialogue is taken.

Scene: Police Court. Speakers: His Honor and an Obeah-struck negro.

"Do you know this person to be an Obeah man?"

"Yes Massa; him catch shadow for true."

"What do you mean by shadow catcher?"

"Him hab coffin. Him set for catch dem shadow."

"What shadow do you mean?"

"When him set Obeah for somebody, him catch dem shadow and then go dead."

"What is it?"

"Hi, Massa. If you want what cure, him cure; if you want what kill, him kill."

Indeed, in a country comprising only four thousand two hundred square miles with a black population of six hundred thousand and but fourteen thousand whites, it is simply wonderful that African superstitions and rites have not been better preserved. That they have become merely a worship of charms, without tendency to ferocity as in the neighbor island of Haiti, must I think be due to constant good example of the whites and conviction among the masses that their best friends, their trusty guardians, must always come from the superior race. Although suffrage is universal and the blacks understand precisely what they are doing when casting ballots, the legislative council members elected are always white men.

Port Antonio is also a famous place for shipping bananas and is the home of an indomitable Yankee named Baker, who has made a fortune out of bananas and grit—the latter quality apparently having been his chief capital. It has a beautiful harbor split in twain by a projecting tongue of land that holds upon its white tip a red and white striped lighthouse, with some attractive residences farther back. Near the village a considerable stream, Black River, makes its way into the sea with much fracas, but is useless for navigation. Upon its banks is a village of Maroons, called Moore Town, which is perhaps the last collection of these descendants of original Indian tribes that owned the island when the Spaniards came. They have ever been brave and fierce warriors, only kept in subjection by overpowering force, and are even now occasionally difficult to manage. Less than a hundred years ago, in 1795, they were sufficiently powerful to declare war against the English, and defeat a force of four thousand five hundred soldiers sent against them. It was found necessary to employ Cuban blood hounds to track them, and, far more appalled by the ferocity of these brutes than by soldiers they surrendered, were deported to Sierra Leone, where they are said to have lived quietly. But they did not all go; for here and elsewhere there are remnants of their race scattered over the land.

Once on a time, when Maryatt's sea stories were in every one's hands, "Tom Cringle's Log" was one of his best. Since going to Jamaica I have often wondered at its local correctness; for, in many points it is still the best guide-book of the island yet extant. Here is "Manchineel," for example, and the "great house at Murton," where the sailor was carried an invalid. It still stands intact and one may travel in every direction by Tom Cringle's chart, without finding much change needed in sailing directions.

We came next to Folly Point, eastern extremity of the island, and turned our prow again toward Kingston. There were but two more ports of call, mere outlets for beautiful St. Thomas-in-the-East, whose hills and valleys made sweet pictures for us all the falling day as we steamed by, or ran in to see who cared to come along. White points of coral reefs showed clear through transparent sea; gaily colored fishes swam deep or sprang into air in play as we swung past, and slowly a westering sun sank behind far away Blue Mountains gilding their summits with celestial fire, or painting them with tints whose beauty was beyond copy.

Our journey was done. As Port Royal lights disappeared, and Kingston wharves were reached, I stepped ashore to find friendly greeting waiting, with a drive over level roads doubly pleasant, after seven days of sea, and agree with my courteous host who says that " Doctor Arden," so Jamaicans call the coasting steamer I had just left, " seems to have been successful in your case, old fellow, you look decidedly better."

So if my readers some day escape Northern winter's cold and find their way to this charming island, it is with sincere conviction that I assure them that a week in Doctor Arden's hands will not only commence a cure, but will give to them the best possible means of forming a general estimate of the history, capacity and resources of Jamaica.

Chapter XII.

CUBA.

TO speak of the Queen of the Antilles as a health resort and be exact, I find it necessary to begin my remarks with the statement, that if it is a health resort in truth, it is only because of its delightful and varying climate, and not in any way due to the social conditions of the country; for within the last twelve years the continued grinding exactions of the Spanish government have so far destroyed the internal resources of the island by exacting taxation and systematic repression of all that is good, that it is no longer a pleasant thing for a traveler to visit Havana city, and practically an unsafe thing for him to do to attempt to travel inland, away from a railway.

This condition of things has been steadily growing worse for five or six years, and during the last winter several who visited Havana told me that it was the custom for men to go about the streets at night only in parties of two or more, well armed and ready for any attack.

This state of affairs is one which is not conducive to quietude of the nervous system, nor to improvement in health of an invalid; therefore, while I propose to describe this beautiful country, and do it full justice in this work, it is with the reservation that its availability and comfort apparently lies in the future, when there may dawn for this most oppressed land an era of freedom and prosperity to which its natural advantages fairly entitle it, and from which it will be divided as long as the Latin race is permitted to retain possession of it, or the Spanish flag to wave over its Havana headquarters.

Cuba is in itself almost a continent. Stretching from a point some sixty miles west of our Florida Keys, to a distance of seven hundred and fifty miles east, with a

THE MORRO — HAVANA.

breadth of from thirty to one hundred miles, it comprises in itself a sufficient amount of territory to give opportunity for journeyings and excursions innumerable. Besides this there are mountains in the eastern part of the island which are high enough to permit of any variety of climate being found upon their soft, sloping, verdure-clad sides. Extensive meadows, plains and valleys, alternating with deep and gloomy gorges, open from the base of island mountains and give to an artist eye a succession of exquisite pictures. On the seaward side slopes are more precipitous, and come down to the water in craggy descents that are picturesque in the extreme. The eastern end of the island is filled with precious metals and valuable minerals, which are at present beginning to be explored by enterprising Americans.

Rivers are few and of but slight extent, because the rocks on which soil is built are mainly limestone, perforated in every direction by rifts and caverns, into which surface water finds ready entrance. In the middle of the island vast plains of red clay resting upon a subsoil of rock, extend from one side to the other, and the population is sparse. Through this section, where once beautiful coffee and rich sugar estates covered every mile, devastations of the Spanish soldiery, volunteers, and banditti have so completely destroyed the value of land to live upon, that only desolation reigns where formerly was wealth and prosperity.

To the westward is the land adapted for the production of coffee, which means a better drained section than we have just left, and still west of that, the vast tobacco plantations in the district of Vuelta Abajo. This belt is eighty-four miles long by twenty-one broad, and comprises the section upon which grow the most valuable specimens of tobacco plant in the world. All the cigars of the great makers of Havana come from this belt, which, while it has never been large enough to supply the immense demand, has not failed to give to millions of cigars made thousands of miles away from it its famous and well-known name.

There is no reason why a tourist visiting Cuba should carry any other money with him than American, which is always at a premium, even over Spanish gold. For bad sailors a good way to reach the island is by rail to Tampa Port, thence by steamer across a smooth sea about twelve hours wide; or one may go direct by the excellent steamers of the Ward line, which sail weekly, and carry one to the entrance of the beautiful bay in four days. By whichever route one comes, he will be landed from the steamer at the custom house dock by boats that ply about the harbor, and will pay whatever amount his limited knowledge of Spanish permits him to bargain for, or the conscience of the boatman allows him to ask, in the latter case, an unknown quantity : the proper fare being twenty-five cents for each person. There is never any trouble at the custom house. Officers are polite, and baggage is fairly on its way to the hotel before the tourist has ceased to be amused and entertained with the strange sights about the dock.

ON THE PASEO

There are several excellent hotels in Havana, the best of which are the Pasaje and Inglaterra, and it is better to have had one's rooms engaged beforehand, as they are frequently crowded during the winter months. A note addressed to Mr. Smyrk at the hotel Pasaje, will meet with prompt attention and insure comfortable quarters. The price of hotel living in Havana is considerably higher than in the other islands that we have visited. It is usual to pay five dollars a day, where, as we have seen in other places, the average is but two. The best rooms in all these Cuban hotels are highest up, and if you can get yours upon the roof, you will be sure to have plenty of fresh, pure air, and the loveliest sunrises in the world. Winter temperature is 77°, running down in the interior to about 75°; but I have repeatedly seen a drop take place to 55°, when everyone, Northerners included, was about half-frozen. Rains are uncommon and rare during the winter months, and frost, of course, is totally unknown, except upon the tops of the highest mountains; yet it will not do to wear thin clothing in Cuba because of frequent severe and sudden changes, and it is better to provide woolen underclothing and flannel suits.

Umbrellas are an absolute necessity. Not so much for rain as for the constant heat of the sun, and a native would as soon think of leaving his house without a hat as without his umbrella.

It is well to be careful of one's diet, for the temptations at the well-furnished tables of these hotels in the shape of savory Spanish dishes and excellent Spanish wines are great. One good meal a day—the breakfast—served at noon, with a moderately light dinner at seven, is quite sufficient for the full-blooded Northerner, who exchanges his winter at home for the summer of Cuba. And if caution is needed in eating, it is much more necessary in drinking. Stimulants should be totally avoided, or indulged in with extreme caution. Here, as elsewhere, I believe it to be much the best plan to bring one's diet as close to the native standard as possible. Be satisfied that the experience of a people in the land which they have inhabited for hundreds of years, will certainly guide them properly, and it is only fair that their example should be followed by those who come to stay but a little while. These dwellers under the sun know better than to increase the caloric in the atmosphere by pouring liquid fire into their stomachs. Their drinks are called "refreshers," and are so in point of fact. Orchata, naranja, guanabana, pañales and limonada, are some of the Spanish names for delicious fruit beverages, served up in immense glasses half-filled with tinkling ice, whose music itself refreshes in this hot climate. One drinks them continually, imbibing through the day a quantity of fluid which would be simply out of the question in a colder land where transpiration through the skin is slow. Our thirsty friends like them all, and are ever on the alert to find something new. Best of all perhaps, is the juice of the green cocoanut, always cool, healthy and cheap.

A Cuban drinks water in a handy sort of way. He takes the jar in his hands, holds it above his mouth eight or ten inches, and pours a stream down his throat that seems to go straight to the bottom of his stomach. It requires practice to do this and not get wet. I tried it, and immediately proceeded to my room for dry clothes. Tumblers work better for foreigners.

In a work of this kind, to speak of Havana and omit all mention of bull fights would manifestly be unfair, and yet the sport is so essentially bloody and cruel that it is better to spare my readers details. Any one who wishes to assist may readily find a chance if he is in Havana over Sunday, for there are few of the Sabbath days when there is not a fight going on at the bull ring across the bay at Regla. I have rarely found Americans who could sit through the spectacle, and not be turned deadly sick by the bloody brutality which these people are pleased to call "amusement."

One visit to this circular butcher's shop is usually sufficient for most of our people.

In many instances careless of human life and reckless of bloodshed, the Habañeros evince a loving care in poverty and distress which gives a stranger a better idea of their character than he would be likely to form on a superficial inspection. Around the ring of the Plaza de Toros, women and little children form a part of every audience, and watch with delight the frightful cruelties of the fight. In war men are massacred on both sides like wild animals, and no quarter is given or asked.

But there are opposite sides to Spanish character. Let us look a little at the better part, and visit two of the leading charities of Cuba, which would do honor to any country on the civilized globe. My excellent friend, Dr. Burgess, who has long represented the medical profession in Cuba, and whose extended residence there has given him great influence in Havana society, accompanied us one day to the well-known Casa de Beneficencia, or Foundling Asylum of the city, where more than a thousand children are constantly cared for. About a mile out, through the seaward streets, we came to an inclosing wall of yellow stone, and with the doctor for guide, passed within the gates. Outside was the lonely street facing the sea, with a few Chinese loitering around; within was busy, bustling life and work. The superintendent was especially anxious that we should see everything, and there was nothing unworthy of careful attention. Within those yellow walls was all the machinery of a town. Shops in which there was for sale every needful thing; streets of handsome buildings; chapels, altars, gardens and fountains, all showed eager activity. We were shown suites of comfortable rooms, where women, poor or rich, married or single, might come for their confinement, and be sure of kind and skilful attention, with no other than voluntary payment, and no questions asked, except name, age, and birthplace. The dining-halls were neat, airy and cheerful, and we saw hundreds of healthy, happy children eating plain, nourishing food to the accompaniment of the church lessons of the day. Then came the dormitories, playrooms, hospitals store-rooms, for all this mass of child life of from a few hours experience in the world to fourteen years of age, when they are apprenticed out to some trade, if not otherwise provided for. This great charity has been endowed by bequests till it is nearly self-sustaining, and is doing more to suppress the infamous crimes of infanticide and abortion than a thousand penal laws.

A few days later, again in company with Dr. Burgess, we devoted half a day to a visit and inspection of the Leper Hospital, the well-known Lazaretto of Havana. All the islands of the West Indies are more or less infested with this terrible disease, which up to within a few months of this present writing, the summer of 1891, has been practically uncontrolled by governmental interference; but within the past year the efforts of a number of determined men have resulted in the segregation of lepers in almost every island where they were known, and the effect of this wise action will be to speedily rid these islands of their greatest curse for tourists — the presence in the streets of victims to this loathsome disease

Dr. Boon, of St. Kitts, who drove me to the newly-built leper asylum at Sandy Point, on that island, which is under the most efficient charge of Dr. Semper, assured me that during his twenty-three years' active work in the island he had neither known nor heard of a single recovery, and this experience but repeats that of every other medical man whom I met throughout the islands. The general opinion, as far as I was able to ascertain it, was against the contagiousness of leprosy. All agreed that, under certain circumstances, it might be transmitted by direct infection, but cases of this kind were so exceedingly rare, that the sisters who have had charge of the lazaretto in Trinidad for twenty-five years told me that they could not recall more than one or two instances where the disease had been propagated in that way.

Havana is peculiarly fortunate in its leper hospital, for it owes nothing to state aid for its erection or support. Many years ago a wealthy merchant, who owned large estates outside the walls, dicovered upon his person evidences that he was a victim to leprosy. There was no place for him to go, no shelter outside his own house, and to remain there involved the health and life of his family, so he built a residence upon these suburban plains and retired to it for life; and, while awaiting death, determined to build and endow a home for all future lepers in the land, to which they could retire upon the appearance of those signs which forever doom a person to a living death. They are not many. A little round, movable mass in the lobe of the ear or under the skin of the face, a slight difference in color of the skin of the hand or arm, and sentence is passed. No pain; no general disturbance of function; only a multiplication of tumors over neck and face, or an extension of paralyzed surface takes place, until the first stage is passed. Then these tumors break down into ulcers, which spread relentlessly until the patient succumbs from exhaustion, unless complications in the way of consumption or some other form of disease puts an end to the scene.

The Havana lazaretto is a great space inclosed within high walls, wherein are two immense stone halls, with well arranged rooms for some three hundred men and women. They are more than pleasant, these wards, surrounded as they are by wide verandahs on every side, and close to the Mexican Gulf, whose salt air breathes coolness and strength into every cranny of every room. They were more attractive than my own chamber at the hotel.

Accompanied by the quiet, sweet-faced sisters who have sanitary charge, we wandered through the building, admiring the pretty gardens, and meeting here and there patients, whose evidences of leprosy were carefully concealed except where the disease had amputated parts of their limbs. It is not impossible to gain access to the Havana lazaretto, and anyone who cares to visit these unfortunates may do so by making application to Dr. Burgess.

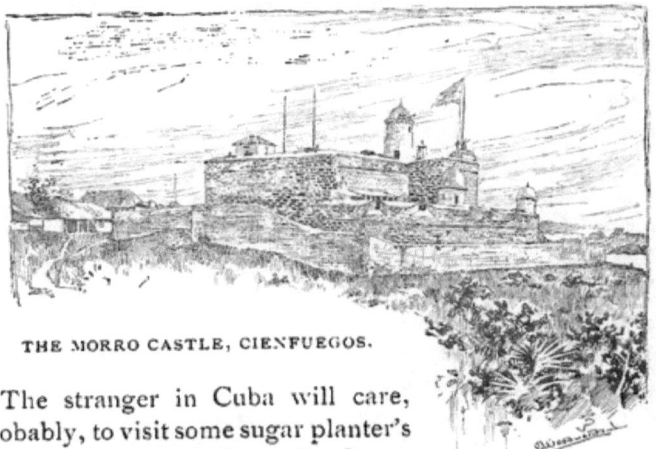

THE MORRO CASTLE, CIENFUEGOS.

The stranger in Cuba will care, probably, to visit some sugar planter's home, or "ingenio," as the Spaniards call it. There are not many sugar plantations within visiting distance of Havana, indeed but one is especially accessible. In order to visit that, considerable diplomatic correspondence is necessary, for it is peculiar to some of our countrymen who travel that they are not content with criticising sharply what they see, but they must print their strictures in some newspaper at home. So when the sugar planter of La Toledo saw himself sneered at in print, and called a "cruel slave driver," he lost his patience, and vowed that Yankees should never come in his gates again.

The excursion may readily be made in one day, and permission to visit the estate can be obtained through the proprietors of the hotel. One goes by cab to the railway station of Marianao, past the beautiful botanical gardens, and by rail to the pretty village, terminus of the road. Carriages must be provided here, to drive across country to the plantation, which is carefully guarded by a well-armed negro, who permits no one to enter without a pass. Driving directly past the works, the residence of the superintendent will be reached, who is always pleased to show visitors about the place and exhibit to them the process of sugar making. The last time that I visited Toledo slavery was still in existence, and there are yet a few of the slaves upon the plantation, but the institution is doomed, and a few more years at most will see its total extinction.

It is well worth a visit, this sugar estate, and for those who have never seen the transformation that cane juice undergoes in becoming sugar it is indeed interesting.

Coffee plantations are practically done with in the island; and this seems a great pity, for the soil of the centre of Cuba is particularly fitted for the growth of the coffee plant; so it is out of the question that a coffee plantation or cafetal can be visited.

An excursion should be made to Matanzas, which may

readily be done in a single day, there being a choice of two routes by rail — one running through the island, and giving a good chance to study its topography for five or six hours; the other, directly along the coast a distance of sixty miles, a run which is made in about two. If any one chooses to remain in Matanzas — and I am by no means sure that it is not a better place to stay than Havana — he will find an excellent hotel kept by three brothers, who are energetic and

MATANZAS ROADSTEAD.

capable, and who manage to make travelers very comfortable at a moderate cost. From Matanzas there are most delightful drives — one to Monserrat, a hill that overhangs the city and the valley of the Yumurri; and another along the beach, through the beautiful Calzada del Mar beside the azure sea, toward the famous caves of Bellamar. There is no more beautiful view in the West Indies than the lovely valley that stretches out from the hill of Monserrat, seventeen miles in length, and eight or ten wide. Winding through the middle is the silver line of the little river that gives the vale its name, bordered on either side by tall palms, whose stately proportions are dwarfed by the distance until they look like children's toys. My only regret in leaving the valley was that I had forgotten my colors, and could not bring a sketch away. I commend Yumurri and its lovely scenery to the thoughtful attention of every artist who goes to Cuba. A buggy carrying two persons may be hired at the hotel for the drive out and back, for about a dollar; or a volante, carrying also two, for three dollars.

Almost every one who visits Matanzas cares to go to the famous caves that have been written about and talked about so much that they are almost as well known as our own Mammoth Cave.

It is a curious story how they were discovered. The land under which they stretch out their winding passages had for many years belonged to a poor planter, who had despaired of ever getting anything valuable from his arid fields. He gave them up finally for pasturage, and one day determined to dig a well to provide his cattle and sheep with water. The workmen had gone down some fifteen feet, when one of them, who was loosening the earth with a crow-bar, felt his tool slip from his hands through the hole it had just made, and fall into unknown space with a ringing sound, as if it struck a metal floor. He climbed out of the well, and went to his employer with the story, who recognized the fact that the crow-bar had probably fallen into some cavern, and at once began to investigate; and the result was the finding of these vast chambers underground, that have been explored a distance of some dozen miles or more, but to which a limit has not yet been discovered.

The drive from the hotel by volante to the caves may be done, and the caves themselves visited, in a half day, at an expense of ten dollars for three persons.

From Matanzas, a railway runs across the island to Cienfuegos; but, unless one is forced to go to this place, I advise that the railway journey be not taken, for it is emphatically the most uncomfortable one that I know of anywhere. There is neither water nor food to be had by the way. At every station one may find readily the rum of the country, and harsh red wines; but no water fit to drink, and it is necessary to take with you on the cars a sufficient quantity of the needful fluid to last until the journey's end is reached.

Cienfuegos is a bright, Yankee-looking town, with two or three fairly good hotels, a pretty square full of flowers, wherein a band plays on Sunday, and an extraordinary club built and owned by Chinese, which is well worth visiting. From this town one may go inland a little way, but not far just now, on account of the banditti, who make life uncomfortable.

The largest city of the eastern part of the island, Santiago de Cuba, is totally useless as a pleasure or health resort.

STREET IN SANTIAGO.

SANTIAGO HARBOR — LOOKING OUT.

There is no hotel worthy of the name, but one or two second-class restaurants, nothing to see, and nothing to do except to get away, and so I shall not trouble the reader to accompany me about Santiago.

The only additional remarks that I care to make in reference to a visit to Cuba are that I have found it a much more expensive place to visit than other islands where English is spoken, and by no means more comfortable in any way. In choosing, therefore, one's route for a vacation, it may be as well to leave out Cuba — at least, until a more beneficent and liberal government than that of Spain has charge of its internal regulations. A few years ago the Isles of Pines, on the south coast of the island, was a well-known resort for consumptives, and was readily reached by steamer from Batabano. Now, however, the departures of boats are irregular and uncertain, and the rapidly decreasing number of visitors who have gone there has prevented proper care being taken of the hotel buildings, and one can hardly be justified in sending delicate invalids to a place so difficult of access as the Isle of Pines is at present.

The average expenses of a tourist in Cuba may fairly be reckoned at six dollars a day, which may, however, be reduced one third, if he remain quietly at a second-class hotel or boarding-house.

> "Ye tropic forests of unfading green!
>   Where the palm tapers and the orange grows,
> Where the light bamboo waves her feathery screen,
>   And her far shade the matchless ceiba throws.
>
> "Ye cloudless ethers of unchanging blue!
>   Save where the rosy streaks of eve give way
> To the clear sapphire of your midnight hue,
>   The burnished azure of your perfect day!
>
> "Yet tell me not my native shores are bleak;
>   That, flushed with liquid wealth, no cane-fields wave;
> For virtue pines and manhood dares not speak,
>   And Nature's glories brighten round the slave."

Chapter XIII.

BERMUDA.

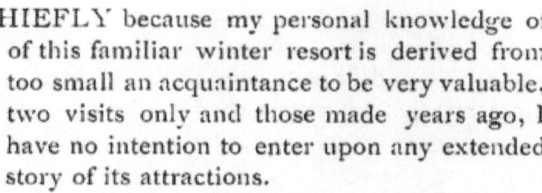

CHIEFLY because my personal knowledge of of this familiar winter resort is derived from too small an acquaintance to be very valuable, two visits only and those made years ago, I have no intention to enter upon any extended story of its attractions.

I had hoped that this chapter would have been written by General Hastings, whose long residence in Bermuda and whose literary attainments furnish an ample equipment for the small task; but an unfortunate attack of grippe prostrated him just when delay in going to press was out of the question, and I must therefore write from such data of my own and other sources, as are at hand. There is but a single route to Bermuda from the United States, and no need of any other, as long as the comfortable steamers of the Quebec line ply as regularly as at present. The Trinidad and Orinoco are excellent sea boats, safe and staunch. Their officers are experienced seamen, and the passage is short, only fifty-five or sixty hours. I wish that I could speak favorably of the beauty of winter sailing on the North Atlantic, but facts are stubborn, and the average passage is a rough one. Perhaps some of the numerous remedies for sea sickness may alleviate it, but a majority of Bermuda passengers spend a large part of the trip in bed, and vacant seats at table are numerous.

Fares are low, $50 the round trip; one has choice of two excellent hotels, kept by Americans, at home rates, or may lodge in comfortable quarters in private houses, at from $10 to $14 a week.

Society is good, and for those who are fond of aquatic sport, Bermuda yachts offer continual pleasure. From the entirely equable nature of the climate, one may arrange ahead for any of the small excursions available, and be sure of having fine weather.

To those whose first visit to warm countries in exchange for a northern winter is made to Bermuda, there is always the delightful fascination of leaving behind a nightmare of cold and wet and dire discomfort, and coming to cheery sunshine, open air, leaves, and flowers that bloom always, serene delight of April temperature, the song of birds that sing every day, and the sense of health which springs afresh each morning that one remains in the enchanted land.

Perhaps one is disappointed, if an old traveler, in the lack of luxuriant tropical vegetation he expected to find; but when he recalls that he is only hours from New York in place of days, there is reason. Coming into port at Hamilton, there are glittering cottages and houses against a sombre background with small elevation, and none of the palm-guarded hills of islands farther south; but once the reef is crossed, inner waters assume such varied tints of transparent blue and emerald green, with many tinted coral shining through, and fishes of rainbow hues darting about, that there is no longer doubt of arrival in the tropics, and each sense is busily occupied in enjoyment of the novel picture. Ashore there is a general impression that time is on the free list, every one has so much of it, and appears to be at a loss what to do with so useless a commodity. Even so small a

ALONG THE BAY SIDE, HAMILTON, BERMUDA.

matter as mooring the steamer to the dock is only accomplished by hours of labor, if any one can be said to labor in Bermuda, for the only real work I saw done there was heavy looking on.

Temperature is comfortable. One is released from fires and winter wraps, except upon rare occasions in morning and evening. But these exceptions are enough to make the rule good that flannels should always be worn next the skin, and woolen outer garments retained. It is better to feel oppressed a little by clothing than by a doctor's bill, and I have seen mornings and evenings in Bermuda when a light overcoat was comfortable.

There are two large hotels, conducted upon the American plan and charging American prices, some twenty boarding-houses whose rates are from $10 to $25 a week, and a few pleasant rooms with private families, where the average visitor may be especially comfortable without the need for such continuous dressing as is the style at the hotels. For Bermuda is becoming a feeble imitation of Saratoga; and the people one sees on the verandahs of the Hamilton or in fashionable dress at its balls or dinner parties, are of the same class that crowds the States or Congress Hall in August and makes merry in hours that should be devoted to rest.

The little islands are coming to have an atmosphere of dissipation and fashion about them that is as welcome to hotel managers as it is distasteful to those who seek repose, moderate prices and comfort in their winter resorts, and experiences of the past winter go to show that lovers of nature and nature's quiet must go farther than Bermuda to find what they seek.

But it is no part of our purpose to criticise invidiously;

and from the number that went to Bermuda this last season, it is plain that it has become popular and will divert a share of American travelers from Florida.

The climate is certainly not warm enough for those who are prescribed heat as a cure. There has been a minimum temperature of 50° F. each winter month for several years, and a daily variation of from 11° to 18°. Now, while this is so vast an improvement over the average weather of the United States, North or South, as to be incomprehensible to those who have never been across the Gulf stream in winter, it does not compare with the steadiness of Nassau, where I have passed sixty days with a total daily variation of 6° from a standard of 70° F., or with the Windward Islands, where there is a total yearly variation of 12° from 80° F.

As a sanitarium, then, Bermuda must be ranked below her sister islands farther south; but as a semi-tropical winter resort for the wealthy it may easily claim first place.

Wheelmen will find with perfect roads and small elevations, constant delight in their machines; and one of them just returned told me that the whole island was like a floor and cycling was at its very best. Delightful journeys may be made to the Natural Arch at Tucker's Town, along the north shore to Pulpit Rock or to see the royal palms at Pembroke Hall, meeting cordial welcome everywhere.

There are no better skippers, better boats, nor better sailing anywhere than in Bermuda yachts, and for those who enjoy the water, every day is pleasant. One needs be a bit of a sailor to feel quite safe in such slight boats so strongly sailed, but accidents worse than spray duckings are almost unknown.

It is essentially a military station, and for those who care

WHERE THE ADMIRAL LIVES, BERMUDA.

for soldiers and their evolutions, there is plenty to do. At the barracks there are always two or three regiments, whose officers are pleasant, jolly chaps, ready for any kind of frolic, and whose drills, guard-mounts, etc., are revelations of discipline to American visitors, whose female contingent never tires of watching their manœuvres afield and never fails to capture as many of them as possible to adorn their little dinner parties and dances afterward.

Take it all in all, Hamilton and the rest of Bermuda will scarcely demand a longer notice than this, unless from the pen of some one far more familiar with it than I; and once more I have to regret the illness of General Hastings and the loss of his facile pen.

Chapter XIV.

NASSAU.

IN the course of our peregrinations through tropical seas, I have reserved my description of Nassau, in the Bahamas, until now, as it is most familiar ground to me, and we are nearly home again when on its shining streets.

This island was my first love, and for four or five successive winters I returned again and again to its delightful climate, its charming home circles of society, and its excellent hotels. Indeed, I became so much attached to the place that it was a matter of considerable difficulty to decide which was most like home to me, this lovely island of the sunny sea or the New England city in which I live.

Nassau, like Cuba, may be reached at present by two ways. One, avoiding stormy sea travel and reducing the actual time on ship board to less than two days, is by rail to Tampa Port, by boat to Havana, rail to Cienfuegos, and thence by the palace steamers of the Ward line direct to Nassau. Along the south coast of Cuba, the last part of this route is sufficiently interesting to richly repay the tourist for all the trouble and expense of the journey, were there nothing else beyond. It is hard to avoid expatiating upon the beauty of this little voyage, and here, if the traveler goes this way, he will have his first view of the Southern Cross. Perhaps he has never seen it before. The chances are he has not, and as everybody is anxious to make the acquaintance of the illustrious stranger, a sufficient amount of determination is easily summoned to meet him, even at two o'clock in the morning. No toilet is needed for the ceremony, as the soft night air of this delightful latitude permits night dresses to be worn on the deck of the steamer at sea.

All the way down, the main object in life of my party seemed to have been a view of the Southern Cross. They searched the whole sky after crosses made of stars, all the way from St. Augustine to Santiago. I pointed out at various times sets more or less crossed, but the captain always said they were false, so I was let alone. But the night out from Santiago they made up their minds that the Southern Cross must be seen, and appeared on deck at two o'clock in the morning ready for an introduction. They gathered around the captain, who pointed to a shining cross on the glistening ceiling overhead, and expressed opposing views as to its effect. There, swinging low among a myriad of sparkling suns, its lower arm almost reaching the haze near the horizon, blazed the constellation, and when I looked at its irregular outlines, that are but half as brilliant as they are farther south, they brought back so vividly scenes in years gone by, of the lovely bay of Rio Janeiro, the River Plate and the palm and coral islands of the South Pacific, that it was like the face of a long absent friend just returned.

It is not much of a cross, artistically speaking; but, then, neither was the one that first made transverse bars emblem of a world's salvation. Of four stars only, and one of them out of line, it makes no great show as far north as this, and needs for its full development of beauty much lower latitudes.

Island after island sprang up and disappeared the whole live-long day; shadows after shadows chased each other along the beautiful mountain sides, and the verdure which

CUMBERLAND STREET—NASSAU.

clothes them to their topmost peaks assumed different colors as the sun went down.

There was no more motion to the steamer in this smooth

sea than upon a river, and the discomfort that attends roughness of the water, was quite lost in the quietude that reigned about.

Morning followed a restful night, but before we came to anchor off Hog Island Light, at the western end of Nassau, the picture framed by the casement of my window was so charming that it is still hard to restrain myself when I talk of this winter island home. A long lowland stretched westward until its dark green was lost in sea: in front, a gray fortress and water battery, with white foam lazily creeping up the slope; to the left a snowy shaft bearing a lantern, and in the centre, the red roofs, spires and many flag staffs of a town that climbed up from the shore step by step to a ridge crowned by Government House, the Royal Victoria Hotel, and a range of handsome residences. Here, there and everywhere fan branches of the cocoanut gave tropical tone, softened and brightened by the tints that are used to color houses and kill the staring white that is so inartistic. There was not one chimney visible, only perpetual summer in the picture, and the motionless silence of the early morning was that of summer lands alone. Restless nerves were quieted; tired eyes looked out upon the scene and found promise of health in the restfulness they saw. Between us and the shore there was the most beautiful water imaginable, some fifty feet deep, of a dark ultramarine blue, changing across the bar to a living emerald green, shaded off by its foam dashing against the beach into snow white, and assuming now and then a tint of gold as morning sunlight fell on it.

Words fall short in describing this beautiful bay, and the truest painter to nature that I know, Bierstadt, in his "Azure Sea" which he sketched from yonder light-house,

PARLIAMENT STREET—NASSAU.

also fell short; and yet, I have heard the picture called a gross exaggeration, a manifest impossibility.

There is no trouble here, or elsewhere indeed, in the West Indies, with the customs. The examination is but a matter of form, soon gone through with, and trunks are rarely opened.

At Nassau there have been one or two new hotels opened this winter, and one may now choose between comparative luxury at the Royal Victoria at four dollars a day, and much smaller prices down to twelve dollars a week, at comfortable boarding houses.

Tourists may choose their yachts either at home or when they arrive; and will find, I think, boats perfectly well fitted for the waters of these quiet seas, at a much lower rate than if they had sent them down from New York in advance, although perhaps not quite so comfortable nor luxurious.

The regulation price for a sail to the sea gardens and return is fifty cents apiece, for a party of not less than five. Over that number or below, a special bargain must be made. Arrangements may be perfected for visits to the out-lying islands, either by the mail-boat, which goes once a week around them all, or by chartering a sponge schooner. In either case the traveler will find it absolutely necessary to provide his own food, and if thereto he adds any article of bedding that he is accustomed to depend upon for comfort, he will go far to insure the pleasure of the voyage.

Horses and carriages are easily obtainable at fair prices; but, as the island government has not established any rate, bargains for everything exceeding a half hour's drive about the town should be made with the owners of the livery stables.

I am delighted to be able to add my tribute to the many which the courteous and kind medical men of Nassau are in the habit of receiving. They have no superiors in any land for skill in the practice that comes within their scope, and are

NICHOLASTOWN — ANDROS ISLAND.

always ready to be the friend as well as the the physician of those whom fortune places under their care.

To all who visit the tropics for the first or second time, the fruits and flowers that they meet are like revelations of dreams. They are so totally different from everyone's conception of them, that a plate of shining fruit that one may buy in the market for a dollar, contains a series of surprises sometimes as unpleasant as striking. I handed a lady one morning a beautiful specimen of custard apple, and, after she had discussed it, asked her what she thought it tasted like. Her answer was: "I do not believe that I shall ever learn to like these tropical fruits; certainly not if the rest that I do not know are as uncomfortable to eat as this one." "Why," said I, "what did it taste like?" "Well," was the reply, "I don't know of anything that I can compare it to, except a ball of cotton saturated with kerosene." While the comparison was a little far fetched, I must confess that many tropical fruits require some practice for their full appreciation.

To those who are fond of fishing, the inhabitants of these transparent seas offer continued delight. They are easily caught in a novel way. One sends his bait down thirty, forty, or even sixty feet, through water so clear that he can watch the bottom as if looking through glass, and see what sort of fish and what color he prefers to tempt with his bait. So he lowers away, past an outlying dogfish, who is watching for something better; past a small specimen of hammer-headed shark, who is keeping a sharp eye on the dogfish, down to where brilliant specimens of squirrel fish or of blue fish are playing over the golden sands below; then, with the utmost deliberation, he places the tempting bait exactly in front of his intended victim's nose, and waits till he takes hold.

Usually the boatman is watching this proceeding through a water glass, and indicates the precise moment when the fish has taken the hook by a sharp command of "Strike, sir, strike." A quick jerk and a pull, and up comes the very fish that you have chosen, to gladden your eyes close by, if, on the way, he is not snapped up by the shark or dog-fish lying in wait.

NATIVE HOME—ELEUTHERA ISLAND.

Shark-fishing parties may be made up after a little notice. In order to make these a success it is necessary that a dead horse, mule or donkey, or the carcass of some large animal should be anchored outside the bar, as ground bait for the sharks. I have seen a dozen man eaters clustering around such a carcass, tearing away at its flesh, or fighting with one another, and have seen fine sport for fishermen in capturing them.

As to the bathing, it is impossible to say too much, or to speak too highly. One feels the need of a few more adjectives when he comes to tell of the beauty of the beach on the other side of Hog Island, opposite the town. Early in the morning before the sun has grown hot, a boat carries a party across the small bay to a little landing, where a narrow path winds a couple of hundred yards through Spanish bayonet and guava bush till it ends in a broad, semi-circular sweep of golden sand, up whose soft incline green, transparent waves creep leisurely, tumbling over each other in rippling laughter. As far out as one can see, this beach of sand floors the azure sea, so transparent that from a long distance any prowling shark may be seen, and his visit avoided. But in the years that I have been here no shark has been seen upon this beach. The water shoals too gradually for them, and with the exception of the early morning visitors for baths there, is no temptation to come. The water is as warm as the blood and beneath the comforting rays of the early morning sun one stretches his limbs upon warm sand with profound delight, and luxuriates in the delicious sensation of the water climbing over his body. It is sparkling with sunshine that it has absorbed all its long way across the Atlantic, and it brings to enervated forms lying prone beneath its soft caresses, some at least of the tonic influences that it has gathered from odd corners of the earth in its journeyings to and fro. From such a bath as this one rises doubly refreshed, stronger in body, more more peaceful in mind, and more quiet in nerves than he he would have believed possible. Such bathing as it is, so utterly unequalled in any of the islands! There is not a place from New Providence to Trinidad; not a beach from Panama to Para, where anything like the same comfort and benefit can be found as on this beautiful sweep of sand at Nassau.

On the hill to the right of the Royal Victoria hotel is an extraordinary structure called "Fort Fincastle." It looks like an old-fashioned side-wheel steamer, and was built with the idea that it might some day be used against an enemy; but it has never done any other duty than that of a signal station, which it at present is. From its bastions one may descend and follow a little path to the right until he comes to the entrance of a curious gorge, to whose floor he may descend by a long flight of steps, known as "The Queen's Staircase," where many people, who fancy that sort of thing, have their photographs taken as souvenirs of the visit.

Another famous evening call and drive is "down along" till you reach Waterloo—an estate on the grounds of which is the pond known as the "Phosphorescent Lake." Our boatman called it the "Preposterous Lake," and when one sees the magnificent display of phosphorescence made by its living waters the name is not so far out after all. Dropping an oar blade into the sleeping surface arouses so much life, scatters so brilliant a display of sparkling light about, that reading a letter or fine print of a newspaper may be easily accomplished in darkest night.

Our boat aroused the inhabitants of the lake, turtles and fishes, which darted here and there in alarm. Every motion they made was clearly defined in lines of flame, which soon crossed and recrossed each other until the surface looked like an illuminated map. From every hand dipped in the water fell showers of gems as it came up again, and where the moonlight shadows were darkest, grasses on the bottom shone through to the top with a steady gleam.

The shouting church at Grantstown is a great curiosity

in its way. It is a square, unpretending building of unpainted pine, with a wattled roof of palm leaves, and a crowd of worshipers whose enthusiasm and religion seem to be about equal. If the visitor is fortunate enough to be present when what they call a "grand rush" takes place, he will see a most curious spectacle, and probably make up his mind that such doings would be better outside the church. The march around while the singing is under way is an exciting scene, and the tune, the very words of the hymn, are ringing in my ears as I write, and they will in yours too, I think, when you hear them. I have put them at the end of this chapter, as they deserve to be preserved.

Nassau, of late, has given considerable attention to the American aloe (sometimes called the century plant in this country), now better known as the Bahama fibre. Governor Robinson, late of Trinidad, formerly of the Bahamas, in his carefully studied and convincing address upon the subject, has so plainly demonstrated the value of this new industry to the island that it scarcely needed the fact of increase of value of some land 1,000 per cent. to tell how great a boon the culture has been to the natives. A young lady of my party this year, bought a hundred acres of land at Nassau, four seasons ago, for the crown price—5 shillings an acre—and refused, this year, $5 an acre for the same. She means to keep it, she says, until it is worth $25 an acre, and believes the time will come soon.

But, after all, the chief value of Nassau, is as a health resort. There are altogether too few amusements,— it is quite too small and dull a place to hold still the eager, healthy pleasure-seeker. I have learned by repeated experience that consumptives, in anything like an advanced stage, do badly there. The climate is so soft and moist that lungs already beginning to soften, go quickly. No such invalid should be sent there; but where bronchitis is concerned, or catarrh of the nasal passages, or any of the many throat diseases that scourge the North in winter, the case is quite reversed. Such sufferers find health in the air, and are frequently cured with a speed that seems miraculous; but the diagnosis must be accurate.

It is, beyond everything, a home for invalids with Bright's disease. I have seen them grow and gain in health almost daily beneath these glowing skies. The skin, whose every

DOWN ALONG.

pore has been closed by cold, rapidly becomes active again, even doubling in some instances its excretory power, and prompt diminution of albumen follows until it disappears. This result persists until following winter comes, and then the patient is obliged to return, of course; but after two or three years, in several of my cases, the improvement was so great that they could stand the cold of the North without serious danger.

In disorders of the nervous system, Nassau is one of the most perfect sanitariums in the world. The regular temperature—neither high nor low, the naturally perfect drainage, pleasant social surroundings, and comfortable quarters, with enforced abstinence from business cares, so relieve the pressure upon over-strained nervous centres that one is hardly ashore before he begins to feel sleepy, and he manages to spend the greater part of the first week in bed with comfort. Then comes a sense of equilibrium to which one has long been a stranger, interrupted only when the mail comes in; then a relapse for a few days follows home news, and improvement begins again when the steamer leaves the bay.

Living is not especially expensive. At the Royal Victoria hotel one may live for $25 to $28 a week; but excellent boarding-houses and private families take guests for about $12 a week.

THE GENERAL ROLL CALL.

Transcribed and Arranged by Mrs. John H. Waterman.

THE GENERAL ROLL CALL.

4 And He fill my soul wid joy and love,
   When de gin'ral roll am called,
      You'll be there!
   And he give my sins a good hard shove,
   When de gin'ral roll am called,
      I'll be there.

5 When de light'ning flash and de thunder roll,
   When de gin'ral roll am called,
      We'll be there,
   Den He'll welcome home your faithful soul,
   When de gin'ral roll am called,
      We'll all be there.

Chapter XV.

THE ORINOCO RIVER.

RINOCO, golden sound! From those early days when Raleigh and Drake were roused to fiery action and deeds of high emprize by stories of the mighty river with its rich mines of gold, its powerful caciques and beautiful women, down to the present, there has hung about the very name of this great stream an atmosphere of mystery and romance.

But little is known of its scenery, resources, or natives; and when it was decided that I should explore its shores for possible health or pleasure resorts, there were few books of travel and no illustrations to which I could turn for preliminary study. Encyclopædias were reticent, and the little book of M. Chas. Gachet, "Excursion au Pays de l'Or," was the only one that gave me any information whatever. So, when my baggage was made ready for the journey at Port of Spain, in Trinidad. I knew so little of the route that it was like commencing a trip to an entirely new land.

Raleigh had told in his letters home, of a grand river in these words: "For I know all the earth does not yield a like confluence of streams and branches, the one crossing the other so many times, and all so fair and large, and so like one another, as no man can tell which to take."

But now many of these mouths are as well known as those of the Mississippi, and are regularly traversed by passenger steamers, whose puffing pipes and screaming whistles still seem strangely out of place amidst the grand silence that Nature keeps in her vast solitudes.

Beyond their depths that are inaccessible to any men save native Indians, there are towns and rich estates, gold mines, and a large population whose wants demand consideration and receive it, not from the government that holds sway over all the river's territory, nor from the island whose commerce is largely to its shores, but from the hands of an enterprising American, who saw a profitable business there and embarked his capital in it.

Mr. Lee's contract with the Venezuelan President, who is the law, provides that he shall transport mails free, Venezuelan officials at half price, and soldiers at one-sixth the rate. This he has faithfully performed, and is now looking for a change in some unforeseen way that will restore his privileges, which were arbitrarily suspended last year.

As I write this, the 1st of March, 1891, there is some prospect of an overturn of government in Venezuela, and what will come afterward no man can tell. Revolution is imminent, unless the wonderful sagacity of Guzman Blanco is great enough to stretch across the Atlantic, and prevent such bloody scenes as have frequently disgraced his country.

The Bolivar, a staunch paddle steamer of about six hundred tons, was built in Wilmington expressly for this trade, and is an excellent specimen of Amercan river steamers. Her cabins are clean and comfortable, and when I was shown into mine by my handsome friend Captain Mathison, prospects for a pleasant trip were excellent.

We left Port of Spain, Saturday evening at six o'clock,

and nearly came to grief at the very start. Every Venezuelan who starts on a journey has a party of friends to see him off; and our arrival on board, the signal for immediate departure, was also the beginning of a sharp struggle on the part of all these friends to get ashore. The steamer lay half a mile from land and a dozen shore-boats shoved into each other to reach the gangway, every boatman shouting for his passengers, every passenger pushing to get to his boat, until in the struggle our boat was nearly capsized. All this seems a trifle, but ground sharks are by no means trifling customers, and the harbor is full of them.

We were more fortunate, however, than to give them a meal, and wound our way amongst the anchored ships toward the Orinoco. The night came swiftly down as usual, and a full moon held forth a greeting hand with shimmering fingers of fire that trembled along the surface of the gulf in sign of welcome.

There is something almost uncanny in the brilliance of a tropical full moon. One can read fine print by its light as well as in a northern summer twilight, and it seems swung far lower and nearer than at home—a silver globe amongst the glittering stars.

One by one the lights of Port of Spain were hidden by the increasing miles that lay between us, until at last mountain outlines and deep-blue sky grew together and were one. Past San Fernando town and the pitch shores of La Brea we steamed on, and when at last I went asleep, there was only shining water visible below and shining worlds above.

The next stateroom to mine was occupied by a family of indefinite numbers and pronounced wakefulness; but I forgave the chattering children who awoke me at five o'clock, at the first look outside. Close to my cabin window, not forty feet away, a lovely panorama was passing; successive scenes of dense jungle of unknown plants, whose intertwining limbs dipped fingers in the swift river, tall palm trunks of silvery white in the moonbeams, and leafless branches of dead trees that were covered with blossoming orchids of marvellous beauty.

Behind, these black recesses stretched away into the virgin fields, whose depths no human foot has ever trod, where cayman, ape and many a brilliant bird live in friendly converse with their kind.

It was scarcely light; yet all these animals were astir, and made themselves audible in calls—some musical, some harsh, all utterly unknown and strange.

Even at this early hour the air was pure and clear. No fog obscured the coming day nor aroused grim fears of malaria, and a shower passing made it pleasantly cool.

As the day came on, the peculiarities of the river showed themselves. No sign of life was visible; indeed, there is none except now and then stray bands of Guarauno Indians, who come to the banks for fish, and occasionally build their huts upon them during the dry season. From bank to bank the stream averages half a mile in width and fifteen feet in depth. The water is loaded with yellow mud, even when low and in dry season as at present; what vast quantities of soil come down with its current in the winter, when it rises from forty to sixty feet perpendicularly and flows at the rate of from six to eight miles an hour, the shallow Gulf of Paria, which is its basin, well shows.

Then these shores, which are even now scarcely out of water, are buried beneath the flood that sweeps over an immense expanse of country in its resistless flow, and the town of Ciudad Bolivar, now at the top of a sandy hill with stone piers half-way up, is brought to the water's edge, and passengers disembark in town instead of on a hill that is in the river bed half the year.

For a hundred miles the banks remain unchanged, and the steamer stopped at a village named Barrancas, a miserable collection of huts, mostly built on the economical plan of four posts and a roof. A group of natives gathered on the steep bank as we slowed down, but no one landed or came aboard, and we pursued our way steadily. About noon, the small breeze that had tempered the heat died away completely, and the mercury climbed up to 93° in my cabin, a poor place to stop long in, although the deck was not much better.

A few miles farther on, the scene changed. The river grew wider and deeper, distant mountains broke the horizon's level, and a series of pretty pictures passed in review. Still there was no sign of human life; and all the day long, save when we stopped at the village, a stray cayman or Indian in his canoe were the only living things we saw.

But these were alive and active enough to make up. Not even in the Ganges or the Nile do saurians attain such immense size as here, although their diet must be wholly of fish. As the steamer rounded a sudden curve, I saw upon a sand-spit, that put out into the stream half a mile or more, what seemed to be a great brown log, caught there when the water fell; and remarked to the captain that it was curious how so large a tree could be felled by the natives.

"Tree!" he shouted. "Give me my rifle, quartermaster!" and *ping* a bullet went shoreward. It struck the log with a spat, and a great monster slowly raised its bulk on four short legs, opened wide a mouth of portentous dimensions, and deliberately slid into the water, the largest cayman of the trip.

"Caramba!" said the captain, "he must have been forty feet long!"

A little later, a commotion in the water close by showed up head and neck of a great, green, crawling lizard, an iguana, from whose savory flesh both whites and natives make nutritious food. He must have been six feet long at least, and I took a shot at him, hitting square in the head—a death wound. In his flurry he threw half his body clear of the water, showing a brilliant green skin, covered with knobby excrescences that looked like warts, and his open mouth was decorated with strong rows of sharp, white teeth. Ashore, these animals snap at a man like a bull-dog, and hang on as hard. So our day was not totally uneventful, even if men were rare.

At eight in the evening we arrived at Las Tablas, the nearest port to the famous Callao gold mines, which were for several years among the most productive in the world. Of late, however, their yield has been falling off, until the price of shares that paid ten dollars each per month upon a par value of two hundred dollars, has dwindled down to one dollar. The decrease, it is said, is due partly to a change of management and partly to a contraction of the vein of ore. Shafts have been sunk only to the depth of eight hundred feet, however, and it is expected that as they progress more will be obtained.

The gold was brought aboard in four boxes, each containing two bars of a thousand ounces tied up in gunny cloths, with a wooden buoy attached in case of an accident coming off to the steamer. They were thrown down on the cabin floor with apparent carelessness; but two well-armed men watched the treasure carefully all night, and in the morning it was to be landed at Ciudad Bolivar, in transit for Caracas, where it is coined.

When the morning came, as it does down here, almost with a bang like Pat's sunset, the steamer was tied head and stern to volcanic rocks half imbedded in white sand, alongside a steep hill of the same, some sixty feet high. Up and down its shifting side a few disconsolate donkeys were climbing, carrying grass upon which to feed the rest of the day; and at the top a dark wall stretched along the town front, showing above it a few yellow-walled flat-roofed houses. And that is all that is visible at first glance of the fourth city of the Venezuelan republic.

After this difficult hill was surmounted the town developed into a rambling lot of streets upon a series of hills, the highest one crowned by a cathedral church and a pretty little square containing one fair bronze statue of the great Bolivar, and four wretched ones, representing the four countries that owe their freedom to his statesmanship and valor.

Shops are large, numerous and well stocked; especially for a place whose merchants pay a hundred per cent. duty, and where no one can do business except by permission of the State. The streets were paved, and there was no external appearance of poverty.

But through the pavement grass was growing; on the the main street were ruins of a horse railway abandoned for lack of business several years ago, and customers for the goods in those wide stores were not. Only rarely was a wheeled vehicle visible; indeed, except about the jail, where red-capped soldiers kept guard, the streets were almost deserted, and everywhere was an air as of a town whose day had been, whose prosperity had vanished.

A few lines in the "Patriota," the daily paper of the town, announced that the editor and senior director had been imprisoned for expressing their opinions too freely upon public questions; and I learned that it was possible that they might remain for months, or at the President's will. Uneasy is the hand that wields a pen where autocrats reign, for so constant an occurrence is the imprisonment of any one who criticizes the Venezuelan government, that opposition newspapers have an attaché called "the prison editor," whose especial duty is to shoulder all responsibility for offensive articles, and spend such time in jail as may please the powers that be.

A chat with my friend of the "Patriota," who was just then in limbo, showed that he regarded his incarceration as quite a regular thing, and was in no way cast down thereby.

There are no curios to be found, no sights to be seen. All amusement that is not sternly supervised is gambling, and that goes on everywhere, baccarat being the favorite game, at which I saw a lad not more than sixteen, win a hundred and fifty dollars in an hour. When the "Santos Dias" (Lent) is done, there is an American circus coming; and I pity acrobats where the mercury is steady at ninety degrees. But there is one thing enough to repay the journey hither: the majestic Orinoco. Standing on a street corner that overlooks its bed a hundred feet below, there is a view for many miles up stream, and one no longer wonders at the enthusiasm with which Spaniards first looked upon its mighty flow, the love their descendants bear for it still. It was low water when I looked down the steep sand-hills to its edge, yet the stream was nearly a mile wide, with banks of brilliant green, and a golden yellow tide.

What must it then be when steamers whose upper decks

UPPER AMAZON AND APURE RIVER BOATS.

are forty feet below, and five times as far away, come directly to the city front, and moor to rings in a wall that is now high in air above the river? For the tide rises in rainy seasons as much as fifty feet, making rivers of brooks, extending navigation a thousand miles inland to Bolivian towns, and bringing produce from even the Rio Negro to civilization and to sale. At this season, March, the steamers Apure and Libertad are useless for want of water, although they only draw four feet; but when November comes, they search the upper country through for trade, and usually with success.

I was particularly desirous to find some specimens of Indian feather work from those upper rivers, for they make hammocks that are beautiful enough for royal museums. But not one remained, and my kind friend, Captain Mathison, was finally forced to acknowledge that even he could not find one, at least this side of the Andes.

Back of the city there is a lagoon that looks like a congenial home for fevers, caymans, and other pestiferous things, and there was no inducement to a closer visit.

Outside the city line, drawn sharply where the red clay ends across this desert of white sand, there is nothing. Only great ox teams traverse these wilds — teams of sixty and eighty bullocks, that carry all heavy machinery and stores to the Callao district, two hundred and fifty miles away.

I do not believe that anyone can fancy what an immense team sixty oxen make, as I saw them ready for a start. They travel ten or twelve miles a day and often take twenty-five days to reach the mines. A single bed-plate for an engine that we brought to Bolivar, weighed five tons, and as the freight contractor receives five cents a *pound* hence to the mines, some idea may be formed of where a part of the money goes.

But upon that wide savannah, that extended its level surface far across country to blue hill-lines that closed the distance, there was a delicious breeze of pure clear air that braced almost like a breath from the sea. We drove hither and thither with no regard to roads — indeed there were none, as on our Western prairies; and took in enough ozone to last all night. Half a mile further, and there is nothing. No human voice, no song of bird proclaims a habitable land, and my friend, the captain, said, "Yes, doctore mio, one must go ten leagues inland before he reaches soil that is worth tilling, or a single home."

Our stay in Bolivar is done, and we begin to prepare for the return voyage; and from this far distant Orinoco town, my steps turn backward, and I am homeward bound.

We brought hither provisions and sundries, as I have said, and in return take beef cattle to Trinidad.

Along the high river banks there were here and there corrals; pens of stakes and withes, into which are counted off a number of beeves to be shipped. We ran up to the shore, built a bridge of plank to the boat, and when all was ready out came a trained bull who lived aboard in state like any other officer. He marched up the hill, stationed himself at the pen entrance, and at a signal, started on a jump for the boat, followed by a herd of half wild and not wholly convinced cattle. Their faith duly clinched by a shower of blows and curses from the drivers, and having small choice in the matter, they were soon securely aboard and the steamer off for another lot.

Such a row as those drivers did make! Screams, yells, curses, and howls came in tremendous volume from their excited throats, somewhat increased, I fear, by the considerate and thoughtful justice with which the chief mate, a

Herculean native, distributed his own attentions. One blow for a bullock and two for a driver, was his idea; and it did seem to work well, for they toiled liked monkeys until the labor was done.

Coming down stream, every hour or so, twinkling lights ashore told where Indian villages — if two or three huts may be so called — had located since our upward trip; and nothing could give a better idea of the purely nomadic character of these indigenes than this sudden total change of habitation. From under the thick greenery of river foliage there came shooting out into the moonlight, canoes, with women paddling hard, to intercept the boat, and men sitting in the bows, lustily shouting the only Spanish word they knew, "Pan, pan!"

And as the only chance these wretches had ever to taste bread was when the Bolivar came along to give them a morsel, we threw them biscuit, which they deftly caught and swiftly vanished with into darkness of deep shade.

They live upon fish and game, using for hunting the blowgun and tiny poisoned arrow, whose smallest puncture is swift paralysis and certain death. Yet my captain tells me that they are happy, jolly and contented; and, if happiness be, indeed, but the possession of everything needed, why should they not be? Viva los Indios!

With all its lacking, with the little that the country has to offer to a tourist, there remains sufficient in the Orinoco journey to tempt a traveler who has not seen South American streams or what a tropical river jungle can show. He will be comfortably housed and fed on board the American steamer Bolivar, well cared for by courteous Captain Mathison and his purser, who speak English fluently, and have something to tell that few people have heard.

And if his journey ends like mine, with a night upon the shining river and of full moon, whose magic light gave transparent beauty to the muddy stream, played marvellous pranks with those black recesses that fancy peopled with strange beasts whose calls are plainly heard, and started him dreaming of conquistador and maiden fair, he will have added to his store of memories afloat some beside which those of Rhine and Danube, Hudson and Mississippi will scarcely hold their own.

APPENDIX.

LEGAL AND CUSTOMARY RATES

FOR

BOATS, CARRIAGES AND CABS

IN THE

PLACES VISITED

APPENDIX.

SANTA CRUZ.

There are no public cabs plying on the streets, but shaky carriages may be obtained from livery stables at the following rates :

For two-seated, two-horse carriage to carry four including driver:
Across the island and return,	$5.00.
Each hour,	2.00.

For one horse, seats for two besides driver:
Across the island and back,	4.00.
Each hour,	1.50.

For any less distance or time, a bargain must be made. As there is no legal rate, coachmen may make their own prices and collect them too unless an agreement with witnesses is made.

BOAT HIRE.

For each passenger to and from the shore, when the ship is at the usual anchorage,	.25.
If alone in boat,	25 cents each way.

There is no hotel at Christianstaat, and meals served at the two boarding houses are poor.

ST. KITTS.

Visitors will find a few shaky cabs stationed around the public square for hire, if by chance any one of them gets so far without having been captured by one of the numerous touters in the shape of negroes, who swarm about the landing quay and in the streets around the public fountain.

There is plenty of time at this island to do all the driving wished; so that it will be wisest to engage horses or a trap for half a day at least, and dinner or breakfast, as the case may be, at a hotel.

There are no legal rates, as far as I could ascertain, but a general custom prevails of charging a certain sum for a certain distance, by those who are in the habit of letting their turn-outs.

> For a single horse and buggy, five or six miles, . $3.00.
> For a double team,"   "   "   . 7.00.

This distance will take a party to the other side of the island, through some of the finest scenery in the tropics to Cayon.

For the longer drive around the island, returning by Sandy Point, thirty miles in all, about double these prices will be charged.

BOATMEN'S FARES.

To or from any vessel lying at anchor in the roads, 24 cents.

Bargains may be made, however, with most of the men, to do the trip both ways for one fare, when there are several in the party.

MARTINIQUE.

There are no public cabs for hire either in this island or in Guadeloupe, and the carriage rates quoted for Martinique will be right for the other French colonies.

Tourists will find livery hacks excellent here, and need be under no apprehensions of being swindled, as all prices are fixed, and no changes made.

CARRIAGES.

Two seat carriage, half-day,		Frs. 15.
" " " one day, .		Frs. 20.
Four " " half-day,	.	Frs. 20
" " " one day, .		Frs. 30.

The fares for a half-day will be sufficient to cover all the ground that the time ashore of a tourist who is to proceed with the ship will allow. A half-day will take him to Morne Rouge, the Fontaines Chaudes, or will show him the city pretty well. As no vehicles are permitted within the Botanical Gardens, and the entrance is a short half mile from the Hotel des Bains, a carriage is unnecessary for that visit, except in case of an invalid.

BOAT FARES.

The usual rate is one franc per passenger and luggage each way to and from the ship. Sometimes boatmen demand two, but a satisfactory arrangement is not difficult to make.

To go to Fort de France, the seat of government, and the location of the famous statue of Empress Josephine, it is necessary to have at least two days, and if the tourist wishes to visit the birthplace of the Empress at Trois Islets, two more.

A steamboat leaves St. Pierre for the capital at 6 A. M., and 4 P. M., running over in about three hours, at 5 francs per passenger, first class, and returns from Fort de France at the same hours. Since the great fire, there is no hotel at Fort de France, so that it is better to make the excursion by daylight.

Monsieur Bediat promises, however, to have his excellent house open again as soon as possible, and then tourists will find Fort de France a charming place to remain in as long as they care to stay.

For Trois Islets, there are fairly good row and sail boats to cross the bay in, but one needs to be a good sailor, as it is often a rough piece of water. From the little town, which contains a parish church where the Tascher family, notably the mother of the Empress, are intombed, to the ruined old sugar mill where Josephine was born, is some three miles; but horses and guides are readily found, and the excursion is a pleasant one. The round trip may be made in one day from Fort de France by starting early in the morning at an average expense of four dollars for each.

ST. LUCIA.
BOAT HIRE.

This varies from 24 cents upward, according to the distance the vessel lies out in the stream.

At present all passenger steamers go directly to the wharf, so that the only need for a boat is when the ship calls during the night for mail or passengers.

There are no carriages for hire at St. Lucia. If any one wishes to go about, ponies may be hired for 50 cents an hour, but the short distances available to tourists are best accomplished on foot.

BARBADOS.

For any hackney carriage, with two or four wheels, one horse:

Fare by distance.

For any distance not exceeding two miles, sixpence for each adult person, and threepence for each child under ten years of age, for each or any part of a mile under the first two miles.

For any distance exceeding two miles:

At the rate of one shilling for each adult person and sixpence for each child under ten years for every mile or part of a mile beyond the first two miles.

Fare by time:

For any time not exceeding one hour, five shillings for one adult person, and if more than one adult, one shilling each; children under ten, half price.

For every livery or hackney carriage, drawn by two horses, one-half extra above these rates.

The above fares to be paid according to distance or time at the option of the hirer, to be expressed at the commencement of the hiring. If not otherwise expressed, the fare to to be paid according to distance, provided that no driver shall be compelled to hire his carriage at time rates between the hours of 8 P. M. and 6 A. M.

But if, after 8 P. M. any cab be found on a stand provided for cabs, the driver thereof may be compelled to hire the same at the rate of ninepence a mile or a part of a mile, not exceeding two miles; if farther, at the rate of one and sixpence for any part of the second two miles for each adult, children half-price.

And for every livery or hackney carriage drawn by two horses, one-half above the rates mentioned.

Night rates as in the case of a single horse.

BOATMEN'S FARES

From the wharf to any vessel at anchor or under way within the bay, when summoned especially.	24 pence.
From the same to the same with one or two passengers and return, fifteen minutes detention,	40 cents.
From the same to the same with one or two passengers and return, thirty minutes detention,	48 "
From the same to the same with one or two passengers and return, one hour detention,	72 "
From the careenage to the engineer's wharf when specially called,	48 "
Same with one or two passengers and return,	60 "
Same, one-half hour detention,	72 "
Same, one hour's detention,	$1.00
For every subsequent hour's detention,	40 cents.
For each passenger above two,	12 "
For landing or taking off passengers with a full boat load of baggage,	$1.00
Same, with a half-load,	72 cents.
For towing a luggage boat to or from any vessel in the bay,	$1.00

All night rates are double.

These are the rates fixed by law, but bargains may always be made with boatmen to carry parties of any number up to six, with luggage, at less fares.

TRINIDAD.

CARRIAGE FARES.

Livery stables charge according to class and style of turn-out. No fixed rates. Charge according to agreement.

Cabs by distance:
For any distance not exceeding one mile, 24 cents.
For every quarter of a mile farther, . . 06 "
Between 8 P. M., and 6 A. M., half more.
Cabs by time:
For any time not exceeding one hour, 96 cents.
For each subsequent quarter of an hour, . 18 "
At night the charge is 96 cents for the first, and 24 cents for each hour after.
Trams, horse cars:
Trams run from 6 A. M., to 10 P. M., at one uniform rate throughout, 6 cents each passenger.

BOAT HIRE.

To or from any vessel lying a quarter of a mile from the custom house dock, one or two passengers, ... 24 cents.
For every additional passenger, . . . 12 "
From one quarter to one mile, two passengers, 48 "
For every additional passenger, . . 24 "
For each additional half-mile, . . 24 "
For each passenger more than two, . . 12 "
Should a boatman take more passengers than his boat is licensed to carry, no fare can be collected.
Double fare if four oars are required. Return is included in the above rates.
Extra for detention at the rate of 48 cents for the first hour, and 45 cents for each subsequent hour.

JAMAICA.

Traveling in Jamaica is particularly pleasant for tourists. Roads are numerous, traversing the island in every direction, giving a constant succession of beautiful views by land and sea, and are kept in perfect order. Railways are short, affording a fair start for the traveler who wishes to do the island; as he will find at the termini carriages to carry him on, and attentive coachmen who know the country and can make arrangements to reach stopping places each night, if the journey be of more than one day in length.

For long distances, where the hirer has continuous use of horses and carriage for several days, it is usual to pay a pound a day for a team to carry two persons with usual light luggage, which price does not include cost of feeding horses or coachman. This may be done either by the stable or the lessee, and there is no special difference which does it, provided it is clearly expressed in the bargain. Unless it is, grain and grass sometimes cost more than the team.

Customary board rates for coachmen are 37 cents a day, and a tip of a daily sixpence beside.

Cab fares in Kingston are sixpence for a mile or under, which is almost anywhere within city limits, and special arrangements for longer distances. Few cabs are to be found on Sunday.

A charming trip, perhaps the most attractive in Jamaica, is made by taking passage in a comfortable little steamer that runs around the island weekly, calling at fourteen ports, with long enough stop at each to give a chance to look about pretty well. Fare for the round trip is $25.00, and it has such a reputation for healthfulness that the steamer is often called by natives the "Doctor Arden." One must be ready to pay no attention to color lines, as three-fourths of the passengers are black, and there is only one table.

Another famous excursion is the ascent of Blue Mountain Peak, an elevation of 7,560 feet, whence a view of the greater part of the island may be obtained and some wonderful sunrises and sunsets enjoyed.

Two days are occupied in making the trip, leaving Kingston early one morning, lunching half-way up, and sleeping on the summit, where a hut has been built for tourists. Food, candles and wraps must be carried on an extra animal. Horses may be hired for the excursion for from five to ten dollars each, or pedestrians may walk as far as Gordon Town and hire animals the rest of the way for two dollars a day. Keys to the hut will be found at Farm Hill House on the way, and it is the proper thing to have your servants make good any firewood you may have burned while there. No scenery in Jamaica equals that on the road to this peak. Tree ferns of immense size, lesser ones in endless and beautiful variety, althea and oleander trees, not bushes, an astonishing array of roses and delicious mountain strawberries, are only some of the attractions.

www.ingramcontent.com/pod-product-compliance
Lightning Source LLC
Chambersburg PA
CBHW031748230426
43669CB00007B/533